DISCARD

ULTIMATE
ATLAS
of *almost* everything

Steve Parker, Sally Morgan
and Philip Steele

Sterling Publishing Co., Inc.
New York

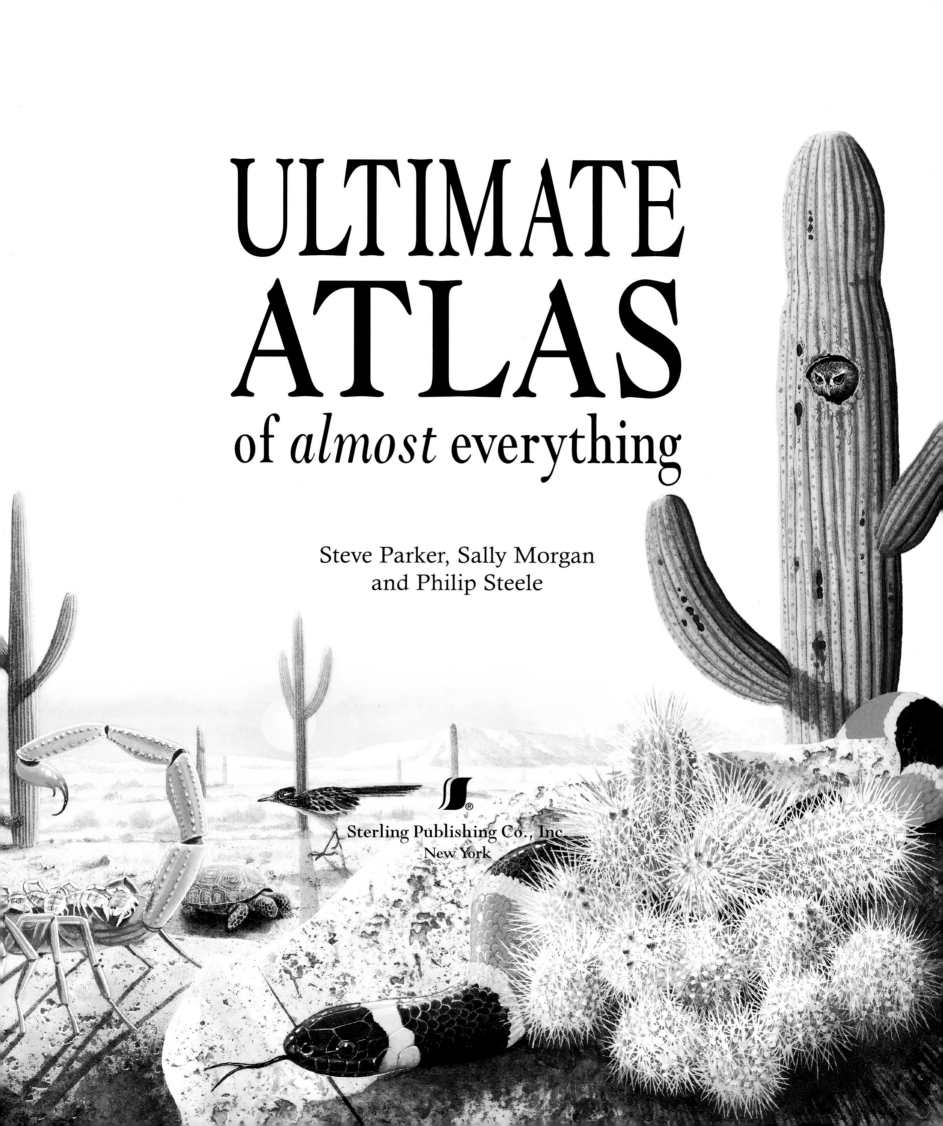

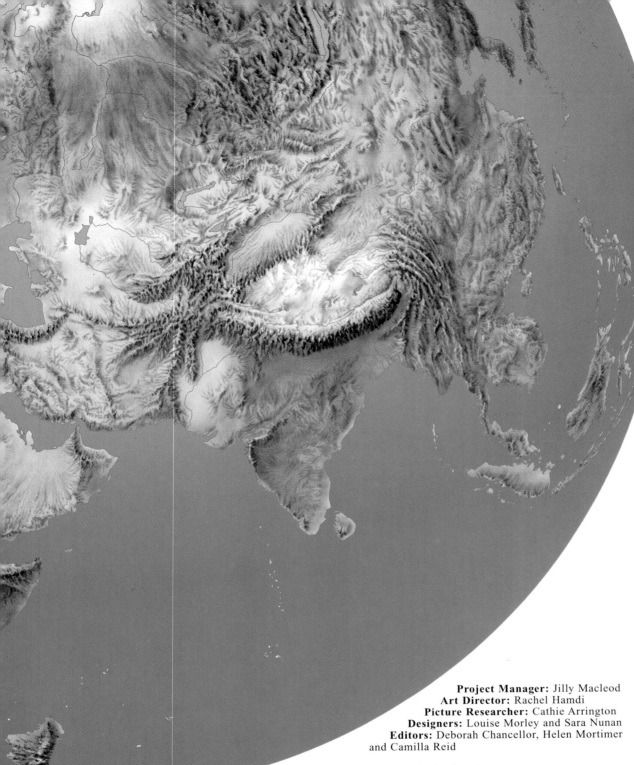

1
PLANET EARTH

Project Manager: Jilly Macleod
Art Director: Rachel Hamdi
Picture Researcher: Cathie Arrington
Designers: Louise Morley and Sara Nunan
Editors: Deborah Chancellor, Helen Mortimer
and Camilla Reid

10 9 8 7 6 5 4 3 2

Paperback edition published in 2001by
Sterling Publishing Company, Inc.
387 Park Avenue South, New York, N.Y. 10016
First published in 1998 by HarperCollins Children's Books,
A Division of HarperCollins Publishers Ltd,
77-85 Fulham Palace Road, London W6 8JB
Copyright © 1998 by HarperCollins Publishers Ltd

Distributed in Canada by Sterling Publishing
c/o Canadian Manda Group, One Atlantic Avenue, Suite 105
Toronto, Ontario, Canada M6K 3E7

Printed in China

Sterling ISBN 0-8069-7759-0 Trade
0-8069-7833-3 Paper

CONTENTS

2
WILDLIFE
OF THE
WORLD

3
PEOPLE
AND
PLACES

4
ATLAS
OF THE
WORLD

1
PLANET
EARTH

Our planet is 4,000 million years old and it is still changing. In one year the Atlantic Ocean widens by a thumb's width, while the Himalayas rise by a thumb's length. Whole continents drift like vast icebergs over the Earth's surface. The Earth has a staggering array of natural wonders – from shooting geysers to cavernous craters – and vast reserves of minerals. But natural forces can also be destructive – volcanoes erupt fiery lava and earthquakes shatter cities in seconds. And today our planet is under threat in other ways – the delicate balance of the environment is disturbed by pollution and natural resources are being rapidly depleted.

Sunrise over Bryce Canyon
National Park, Utah, USA.

THE EARTH IN SPACE

If you look out from the top of a mountain, the landscape stretches away into the distance. Planet Earth seems huge, flat and boundless, but if you compare it to the vastness of space, and gigantic bodies like stars, our Earth is just a speck of rock whirling though the dark emptiness. It is one of nine planets travelling around the Sun, our local star. The Sun, its planets, their moons, and smaller bodies such as asteroids make up the Solar System.

ABOVE: This is a view of the Earth seen by the astronauts of the Apollo 11 spacecraft (the first to land on the Moon) in 1969. The photograph was taken about 112,750mi from Earth, almost halfway to the Moon.

Summer in the South

23°
Axis of spin
Axis of orbit

Summer in the North

Years and seasons
One year is one Earth orbit around the Sun (above). The Earth spins once every 24 hours around its axis, giving day and night. The axis is tilted at 23° from the axis of orbit so, for part of the year, the lower half of the Earth, or Southern Hemisphere, is nearer the Sun – this gives summertime in the South. When it is furthest from the Sun, it is winter in the South.

Solar System forms

Earth is born

Prehistoric Earth cools and hardens

Earth today

The Jupiter Orbiter and Probe, more commonly known as Galileo, was launched on October 18, 1989.

Birth of the Earth
Many scientists believe that a huge explosion called Big Bang began the Universe some 12,000 million years ago. Swirling clouds of dust and space rock (above) gradually clumped together to make the Earth and other Solar System planets, about 4,600 million years ago.

Galileo crossed the asteroid belt between Mars and Jupiter, where millions of tiny rocky "minor planets" orbit.

Jupiter
Diameter: 88,860mi.
Average distance from Sun: 483 million mi.

Space Explorers

The first satellite, Sputnik 1, went into orbit around the Earth in 1957. Since then, thousands of satellites and deep-space probes, equipped with cameras and scientific equipment, have gathered information about planets, stars, comets and other heavenly bodies. In 1995, Galileo (right) reached Jupiter after a six-year journey. It dropped a probe into the dense, swirling gases and sent back information about the amazing conditions inside this "gas giant."

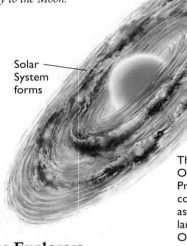

A probe was released down to Jupiter, and worked for about an hour before being destroyed by the planet's atmosphere.

Mars
Diameter: 4,217mi.
Average distance from Sun: 142 million mi.

The Sun's Family

There are two main groups of planets. The four inner ones nearest the Sun are Mercury, Venus, Earth and Mars – they are small and rocky. Beyond Mars is a massive gap occupied only by asteroids, tiny "minor planets." The four outer planets are Jupiter, Saturn, Uranus and Neptune – they are all big and gassy. The ninth and outermost planet is Pluto, a tiny, frozen, rocky world. All the planets orbit the Sun in ellipses (ovals). Mercury has the fastest orbit, at 88 Earth days. Pluto's orbit takes 284 Earth years.

Venus
Diameter: 7,521mi.
Average distance from Sun: 67 million mi.

Earth
Diameter: 7,927mi.
Average distance from Sun: 93 million mi.

Mercury
Diameter: 3,032mi.
Average distance from Sun: 36 million mi.

Pluto
Diameter:
1,365mi.
Average
distance from
Sun: 3,665
million mi.

Neptune
Diameter: 30,750mi.
Average distance from
Sun: 2,794 million mi.

We are
about here

Galaxies galore
Space is dotted with galaxies, which are clusters of
millions of stars, separated from each other by huge
regions of emptiness. Our galaxy (above) is called The
Galaxy or Milky Way. It has a central disc with two long
spiral arms, and the whole galaxy spins around in space.

*ABOVE: Space contains many objects besides stars and planets.
A black hole is a region of matter and energy which has incredible
gravity because it is squeezed and compressed into such a small
place. It attracts and "swallows" everything within reach. Even
light can't get out, which is why the hole is black.*

Uranus
Diameter: 31,750mi.
Average distance
from Sun: 1,785
million mi.

Saturn
Diameter: 74,568mi.
Average distance from
Sun: 887 million mi.

FANTASTIC FACTS

● Our own galaxy
contains about 2,000
million stars – our Sun is
just one of them.

● The Sun orbits the
center of our Galaxy at
a staggering speed of
559,000mi/h, taking all its
planets along with it.

● Launched in 1972, the
deep space probe Pioneer
10 left our Solar System in
1983, becoming the first
man-made object ever
to do so.

Planetary rings
The four giant gas planets all have rings.
Saturn's are the most striking, made of icy
rocks varying from head-sized to bigger than
a truck. Each ring is only about 1.25mi thick.

*BELOW: These star maps name
some of the brightest and most
famous constellations.*

**Northern
skies**

Pisces

Pegasus

Aries

Andromeda

Taurus

Sagitta

Cygnus

Orion

Hercules

Ursa Minor
Polaris (North
Pole Star)

Gemini

Ursa Major

Canis Minor

Cancer

Hydra

Virgo

Leo

Aquarius

Phoenix

Capricornus

Sagittarius

Orion

Scorpius

Canis Major

Crux
(Southern
Cross)

Lupus

Milky
Way

Hydra

Libra

Virgo

**Southern
skies**

Sagittarius

Starry skies
A constellation is a
group of bright stars. There
are 88 constellations, but they
can't all be seen at once – some are visible in the night
skies of the North, others only from the southern skies
(see maps above). As the Earth spins on its axis, the
constellations seem to swirl around the sky. But the North
Pole Star stays still, because it is in line with the Earth's axis.

*LEFT: The 12 signs of
the Zodiac are based
on figures and objects
seen in the stars.*

Sun
Diameter: 863,750mi.
Temperature at core:
29 million °F.

SEE ALSO
Weather and Climate p 30
Polluting Our Planet p 34

CONTINENTS ADRIFT

Our world map is gradually changing. The Atlantic Ocean is widening by about half an inch each year, and the Pacific is shrinking, as the continents move slowly across the globe. This process is called continental drift, and it happens because the Earth's surface is made of about 12 curved pieces known as lithospheric plates. These plates slip and slide, driven by huge temperatures and pressures deep down inside the planet.

ABOVE: Identical fossils found in continents now widely spaced apart suggest that those continents were once joined together. They include plants like this ancient seed-fern Glossopteris, *which grew in South America, Africa and Australia.*

450 million years ago

PANTHALASSA

PANGAEA

225 million years ago

120 million years ago

RIGHT: In some places, lithospheric plates pull apart. The land between them slips down to create a rift valley, such as the Great Rift Valley that runs for 2,500mi through East Africa.

The Changing World

Continental drift never stops – it has been happening for more than 4,000 million years. To follow its progress, scientists have looked at different forms of evidence, such as the shapes of the continents and oceans, and where different types of rocks and fossils can be found. From about 250 million years ago, all the landmasses had drifted together to form one supercontinent called Pangaea. This massive area of land was surrounded by a single vast sea called Panthalassa. Pangaea began to break up again around 200 million years ago.

40 million years ago

Present day

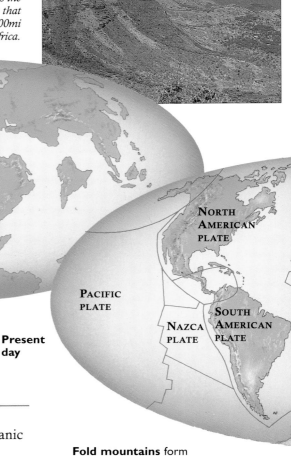

NORTH AMERICAN PLATE

PACIFIC PLATE

NAZCA PLATE

SOUTH AMERICAN PLATE

Fold mountains form when oceanic crust crumples into continental crust. Most continents have been carried around like rafts on their plates for millions of years. It's mainly the oceanic crust around the edge of each plate that changes shape.

Earthquake danger

Where plate edges meet on land, there may be a visible crack, or fault, as seen above. This is part of the San Andreas Fault that runs through San Francisco and Los Angeles, USA. Here, sections of the mighty Pacific and North American lithospheric plates jam together. When the plates slip against each other, as they sometimes do, they cause an earthquake.

Making and Breaking Plates

The Earth has two main kinds of outer layer, or crust. Under the seas is the oceanic crust – this is only about 3-6mi thick. Beneath the land is the continental crust, which goes down 18-30mi. A lithospheric plate is an area of continental and oceanic crust, plus the outer part of the next "layer" down, called the mantle. In total, lithospheric plates are about 50-90mi thick. New oceanic crust forms when molten rock from far below forces its way up between two plates (see right). The hot rock then hardens, adding to the plate edges. This happens at a mid-oceanic ridge, a crack-like chain of mountains on the sea bed. Sometimes, the edge of one plate is forced underneath another plate, making it melt back into the mantle. An area where this happens is called a subduction zone.

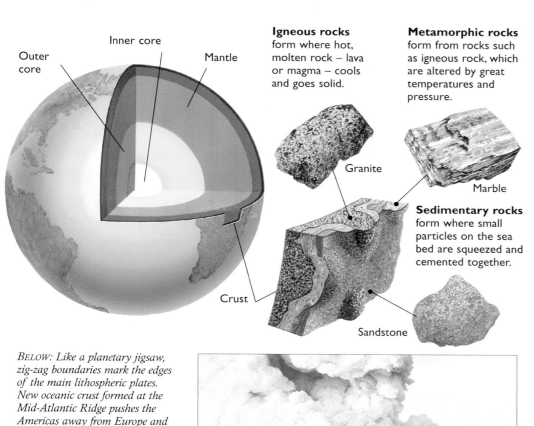

Outer core
Inner core
Mantle

Igneous rocks form where hot, molten rock – lava or magma – cools and goes solid.

Metamorphic rocks form from rocks such as igneous rock, which are altered by great temperatures and pressure.

Granite

Marble

Sedimentary rocks form where small particles on the sea bed are squeezed and cemented together.

Crust

Sandstone

Inside the Earth

Our planet has three main layers (see far left). The crust is from three to 30mi thick, and contains rock types such as igneous, sedimentary and metamorphic rocks. In proportion to the whole Earth, the crust is thinner than the skin of an apple. The mantle is about 1,800mi thick and becomes less solid with depth. The semi-liquid outer core is 1,370mi thick, and the solid inner core is 1,550mi across. Both cores are made up of substances rich in iron and nickel.

SEE ALSO
Earthquakes & Volcanoes p 14
Mountain Building p 16

FANTASTIC FACTS

• The Red Sea is a "baby sea." In 60 million years' time it will be as wide as the Atlantic is today.

• Because of continental drift, the world's entire ocean floor is renewed every 150 million years.

• Fossils found in Antarctica show that this frozen continent once basked in sunshine near the Equator!

• When dinosaurs first appeared, all the land was grouped together as the supercontinent Pangaea.

BELOW: Like a planetary jigsaw, zig-zag boundaries mark the edges of the main lithospheric plates. New oceanic crust formed at the Mid-Atlantic Ridge pushes the Americas away from Europe and Africa, while the Indo-Australian plate is ramming into the Eurasian plate, creating the Himalayan fold mountains.

LEFT: The longest mid-oceanic ridge is under the central Atlantic. At its northern end, the plate edges rise above sea level and pass through Iceland. In the shallow seas nearby, volcanic action and oozing red-hot rock build new islands. One such island is Surtsey, which appeared above the waves in clouds of steam in 1963.

As the oceanic crust melts into the mantle, it gives off "bubbles" of lighter rock. They force up weaknesses and cracks near the edge of a plate, forming a line of **volcanoes**. Many plate edges are active zones of earthquakes and volcanoes.

EURASIAN PLATE

PACIFIC PLATE

AFRICAN PLATE

INDO-AUSTRALIAN PLATE

ANTARCTIC PLATE

A **mid-oceanic ridge** is like a long, thin volcano that stretches across the sea bed. As new oceanic crust forms and the sea floor spreads, the plates are forced sideways. The oldest rocks in the oceanic crust are farthest from the ridge.

At a **subduction zone**, the edge of a plate is forced back down into the mantle. This can create a steep-sided valley or oceanic trench over 6mi deep.

Plate moves sideways

Oceanic crust

Lithospheric plate

Continental crust

Mantle

Massive, slow currents of heat called convection currents are moving deep down in the Earth. These powerful currents force molten rock up through the mid-oceanic ridge and make continental drift happen.

EARTHQUAKES AND VOLCANOES

ABOVE: This Ancient Chinese device was designed to detect earthquakes. When the jar shook, a lever inside knocked a ball from one of the dragons into a frog's mouth. The ball affected indicated the quake's direction.

A violent earthquake shakes solid rock like jelly, opening great cracks in the ground and making cities crumble. An erupting volcano spews red-hot rock, filling the air with choking gases and clouds of ash. These violent events happen where the Earth's crust is thin or cracked, usually along fault lines at the edges of the lithospheric plates. The plates are continually moving past each other. But if two lock, forces build up until suddenly the plates slip, causing an earthquake. Many volcanoes and quakes happen in an area called the "Ring of Fire" which circles the Pacific.

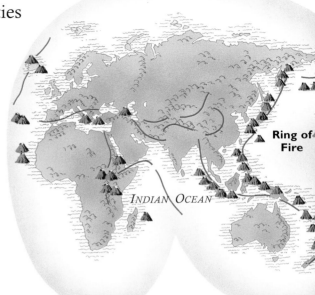

ABOVE: This maps shows the world's active volcanoes and earthquake zones.

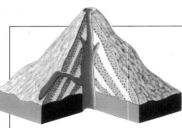

Fault line

Epicenter

Focus

Shock waves

Earthquakes in Action

The energy released during an earthquake is centerd at a point called the focus, which lies deep underground. Vibrations called shock, or seismic, waves spread out in all directions from the focus, first reaching a point on the surface called the epicenter, which is directly above the focus. To us, it seems the quake starts here. As the rock plates slip, the land's surface cracks along the fault line and the ground shudders violently.

The Erupting Earth

An active volcano is fed by incredibly hot molten rock called magma which lies deep below the surface under enormous pressure. The magma forces its way up through holes or cracks – especially between the lithospheric plates – and emerges into the air as lava. The lava may erupt like a huge fountain, or ooze slowly and gently out of the volcano. Landscapes shaped by volcanic action show features that have formed over millions of years. Small "parasitic" cones sometimes grow on the sides of the volcano, and geysers often form near the base.

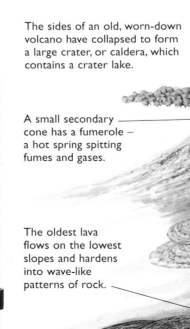

The sides of an old, worn-down volcano have collapsed to form a large crater, or caldera, which contains a crater lake.

A small secondary cone has a fumerole – a hot spring spitting fumes and gases.

The oldest lava flows on the lowest slopes and hardens into wave-like patterns of rock.

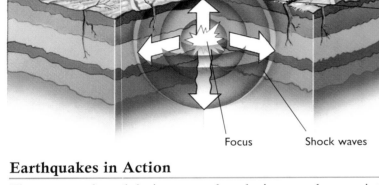

TYPES OF VOLCANO

Volcanoes come in different shapes and sizes, depending on how they were formed. Composite volcanoes are tall and steep, whereas shield volcanoes are wide and low,

A **composite volcano** has many layers formed from thick lava, built up during successive eruptions.

A **shield volcano** forms when thin, runny lava oozes out and spreads widely over a long time.

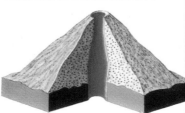

A **cinder cone** is usually small and steep, made of hardened ash, cinders and small lava lumps.

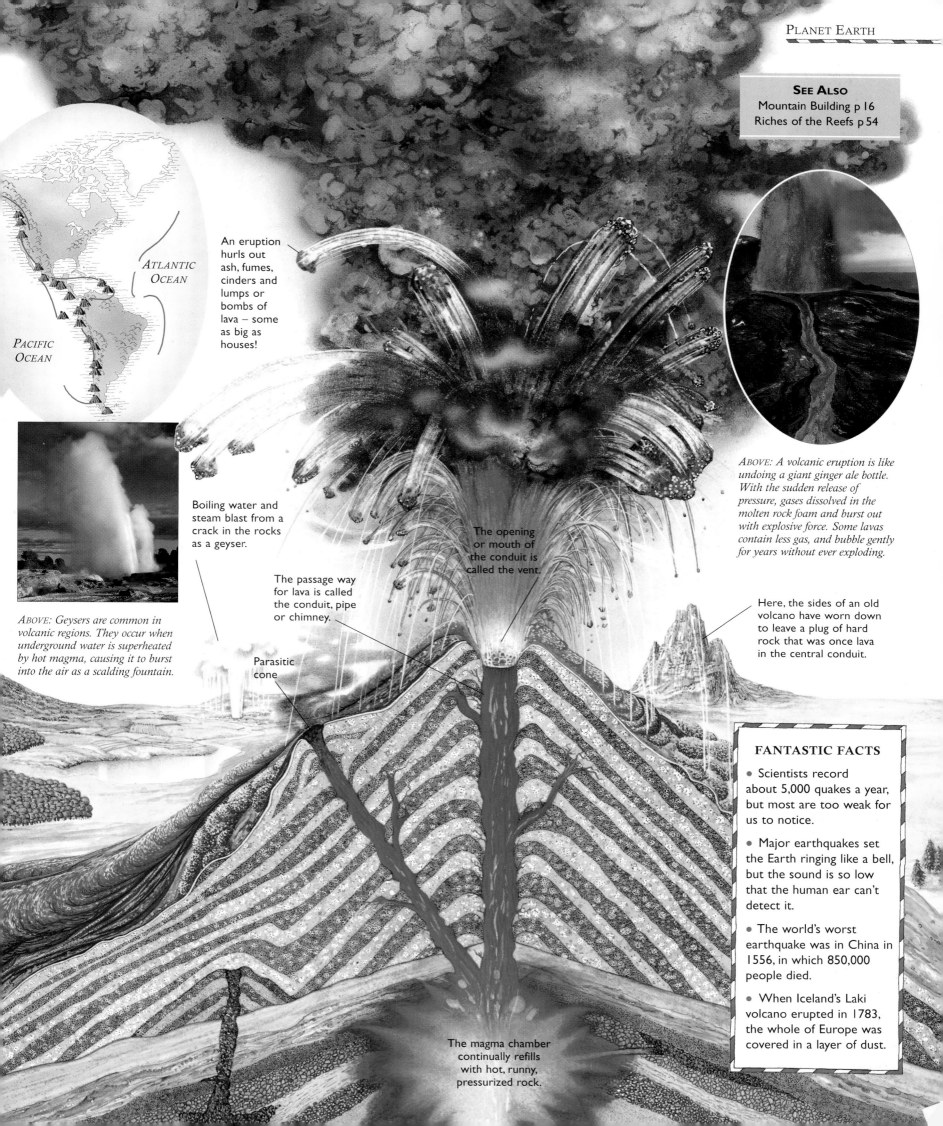

SEE ALSO
Mountain Building p 16
Riches of the Reefs p 54

ATLANTIC
OCEAN

PACIFIC
OCEAN

An eruption
hurls out
ash, fumes,
cinders and
lumps or
bombs of
lava – some
as big as
houses!

*ABOVE: A volcanic eruption is like
undoing a giant ginger ale bottle.
With the sudden release of
pressure, gases dissolved in the
molten rock foam and burst out
with explosive force. Some lavas
contain less gas, and bubble gently
for years without ever exploding.*

Boiling water and
steam blast from a
crack in the rocks
as a geyser.

The opening
or mouth of
the conduit is
called the vent.

The passage way
for lava is called
the conduit, pipe
or chimney.

Here, the sides of an old
volcano have worn down
to leave a plug of hard
rock that was once lava
in the central conduit.

*ABOVE: Geysers are common in
volcanic regions. They occur when
underground water is superheated
by hot magma, causing it to burst
into the air as a scalding fountain.*

Parasitic
cone

FANTASTIC FACTS

• Scientists record
about 5,000 quakes a year,
but most are too weak for
us to notice.

• Major earthquakes set
the Earth ringing like a
bell, but the sound is so low
that the human ear can't
detect it.

• The world's worst
earthquake was in China in
1556, in which 850,000
people died.

• When Iceland's Laki
volcano erupted in 1783,
the whole of Europe was
covered in a layer of dust.

The magma chamber
continually refills
with hot, runny,
pressurized rock.

MOUNTAIN BUILDING

When Everest was first conquered in 1953 it was about six feet shorter than it is today. The world's tallest peak is slowly being pushed upwards, thanks to movements deep down in the Earth. When the huge lithospheric plates that make up the surface of the Earth push against each other, the solid rock at their edges crumples up, creating lines of fold mountains. Other types of mountains are made by volcanoes, or when powerful plate movements squeeze and raise huge blocks of the Earth's crust.

ABOVE: Upheavals in the Earth's surface thrust marine fossils, such as this ammonite, from the sea bed on to the mountain tops.

Flat layers of sedimentary rocks are laid down beneath the sea over millions of years.

① ② ③

Layers of light sedimentary rocks that once lay flat beneath the sea bed slowly buckle and fold under the huge forces created by the advancing plate.

LEFT: The sedimentary rock in these cliffs in Greenland is at least 600 million years old.

The edge of the advancing plate slides below the other plate.

Rock of Ages

Sedimentary rocks are made of small pieces of rock and sometimes fossilized bits of animals and plants. Millions of years ago, these sediments were washed into shallow seas by rivers, where they settled in deeper and deeper layers. Gradually these layers, or strata, squeezed together to form solid rock. Over millions more years, movements deep in the Earth lifted the rocks above sea level, cracking them apart to show the layers. Usually, the lower down the layer, the older the rock.

RIGHT: People who live in mountainous regions, such as this Nepalese farmer, have thick, warm coats – and so do their animals, like this yak.

Mountain Farming

Mountains are wetter, colder and windier than their surrounding lowlands. It gets 12°F colder for every 3,000 feet you climb. The higher the mountain, the thinner the air, and the stronger the harmful rays of the Sun. At high altitudes, farmers are at risk from ultraviolet light and sunburn, despite the cold. The soil is thin, dry and poor for farming, because the wind blows it away and rainwater drains quickly down the slopes.

Folding and Forming

Fold mountains such as the Himalayas are created in a process that takes millions of years. First, sediments slowly build up beneath the sea, turning into layers of sedimentary rocks (1). As one lithospheric plates pushes into a neighboring plate, these light layers of rock are crumpled and folded into higher areas of land, forming mountains (2). The sea disappears altogether. In time, ice, snow, wind, rain and sun wear away, or erode, the softer parts of the peaks (3).

16

Mountains around the world
The map shows the main mountain ranges of the world. Different types of mountains are named after the way they form. Volcanic mountains (below) build up over many eruptions. Block-fault mountains (right) happen where a block of crustal rock slips along lines of weakness called faults. Fold mountains (far right) are caused by sliding lithospheric plates.

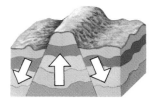

Block-fault mountains are due to crustal plate movements that crack giant blocks of rock, forcing one up in relation to the others.

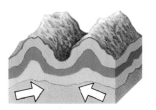

Simple fold mountains contain layers, or strata, that have been squeezed and buckled, but not tipped over.

Mt McKinley
NORTH AMERICA
EUROPE
Rocky Mts
Appalachians
Urals
ASIA
Alps
Mt Elbrus
Caucasus Mts
Himalayas
Mt Everest
Atlas Mts
AFRICA
SOUTH AMERICA
Ethiopian Highlands
Kilimanjaro
Mt Wilhelm
Andes
Great Dividing Range
AUSTRALIA
▲ Aconcagua
▲ Vinson Massif
ANTARCTICA

Volcanic mountains form as layers of hot, thick, molten lava from successive eruptions cool and go solid.

After a period of little motion, one lithospheric plate begins to move towards its neighbor.

Complex fold mountains have such enormous forces and movements beneath them that the rock layers crack, slide and tip right over.

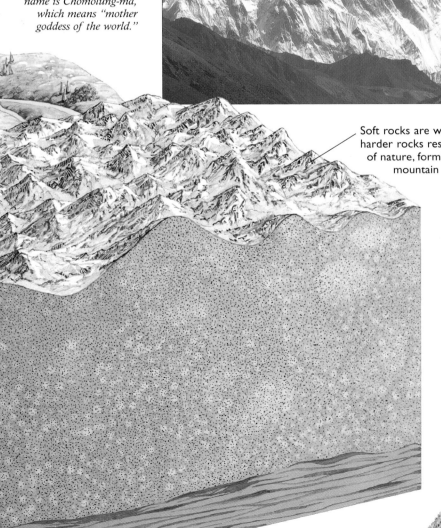

RIGHT: This stunning view from the top of the world shows Mount Everest, on the borders of Nepal and Tibet. The mountain is named after Sir George Everest, who was British surveyor-general in India during the 1860s. Its local name is Chomolung-ma, which means "mother goddess of the world."

Mountain Ranges

The world's largest and highest mountain group is the Himalayas. It stretches across mid-Asia and has the world's 28 tallest peaks, the highest being Everest. Second is K2 or Gowdin-Austen in the Kashmir area, at 28,252ft. The world's second-largest mountain range is the Andes – Aconcagua in Argentina is the 29th tallest peak. Australia is a relatively flat continent, its highest peak being Kosciusko at just 7,313ft.

Soft rocks are warn away, but harder rocks resist the forces of nature, forming jagged mountain peaks.

SEE ALSO
Life among the Peaks p 42
Life in the Past p 58

FANTASTIC FACTS

● From base to peak, the tallest mountain in the world is Mauna Kea, on the Pacific island of Hawaii. It is 33,483ft tall, but only 13,795ft rises above sea level.

● The summit of Mount Everest is not the farthest point from the Earth's center. Our planet is slightly pear-shaped, so the 20,562ft Andean peak of Chimborazo, in Ecuador, is in effect 6,890 feet taller than Everest.

BELOW: The highest mountains in each continent or region are shown here, measured in feet above sea level. Western Europe's highest peak is Mont Blanc in the Alps, at 15,771ft.

Aconcagua (Argentina, South America) 22,834ft

Everest (Nepal/Tibet, Asia) 29,028ft

McKinley (Alaska, North America) 20,320ft

Kilimanjaro (Tanzania, Africa) 19,340ft

Wilhelm (Papua New Guinea, Oceania) 14,794ft

Elbrus (Georgia, Europe) 18,511ft

Vinson (Antarctica) 16,864ft

WORLDS OF ICE

Below 32°F, water freezes into ice. Such temperatures are found in the polar regions, which are farthest from the Sun, and also on high mountains. These areas have hail and snow instead of rain, and are covered in ice. Glaciers are rivers of slow-flowing ice – most spill into the sea from the polar regions. There are also large ice sheets and glaciers in mountains such as the Himalayas, Andes, Rockies, Alps and Pyrenees.

Basin

Upper snowfield

LEFT: Just like an ice-cube floating in a glass of water, a massive iceberg floats in the sea, with only one-sixth of its volume showing above water.

A cirque lake, or tarn, remains where ice has carved out a bowl shape in the hillside.

Slowly Downhill

A glacier flows because snow falling on higher ground gets squashed into ice, pushing the glacier from above. Its speed depends on how steep the slope is. The average rate is less than three feet each day, but the Columbia Glacier near Anchorage, Alaska, slides along 66ft a day. As it flows, the glacier rubs the rocks beneath. These stick in the ice and scrape along like a giant sheet of sandpaper, cutting a U-shaped valley. The picture (right) shows the main features of a glacier, and below is a valley after the ice has melted.

A stream in a hanging valley tips its contents over a waterfall.

Sea of Ice

The Arctic Ocean (below) has an average depth of 4,365ft, and is almost entirely surrounded by land. Even in summer, the center of the Arctic is covered by floating ice sheets, pack ice and icebergs. Most of the sheet ice is less than 32ft thick, so fish, polar bears, whales and even submarines can move about underneath. During the freezing cold winter, the Sun never rises above the horizon, and temperatures drop to -76°F. Ice spreads over most of the Arctic Ocean.

Arctic Circle

North Pole

The valley's sides form a U shape, unlike the V-shape of a valley eroded by a river.

This flowing river is fed by water from a melting glacier farther up the valley.

Large boulders called erratics, carried far downhill by the glacier, lie where they were dumped by the melting ice.

ABOVE: The Norwegian Fjords are U-shaped valleys that were cut by glaciers in colder times.

Arctic Circle

SIBERIA

ARCTIC OCEAN

Permanent sea ice

North Pole

SCANDINAVIA

GREENLAND

Ice cap

NORTH AMERICA

Extent of ice in winter

Kingdoms of Ice

There have been many great ice ages throughout the Earth's history, some lasting thousands of years. Ice ages may be caused by the planet wobbling and changing slightly its angle of tilt as it orbits the Sun, resulting in a change of climate. The last ice age was fairly short, and ended about 10,000 years ago. As the glaciers shrank back towards the poles, they left distinctive U-shaped valleys behind.

BELOW: Polar ice sheets have an eerie beauty, with regular hisses and creaks, and occasional crashes as a section avalanches into the sea.

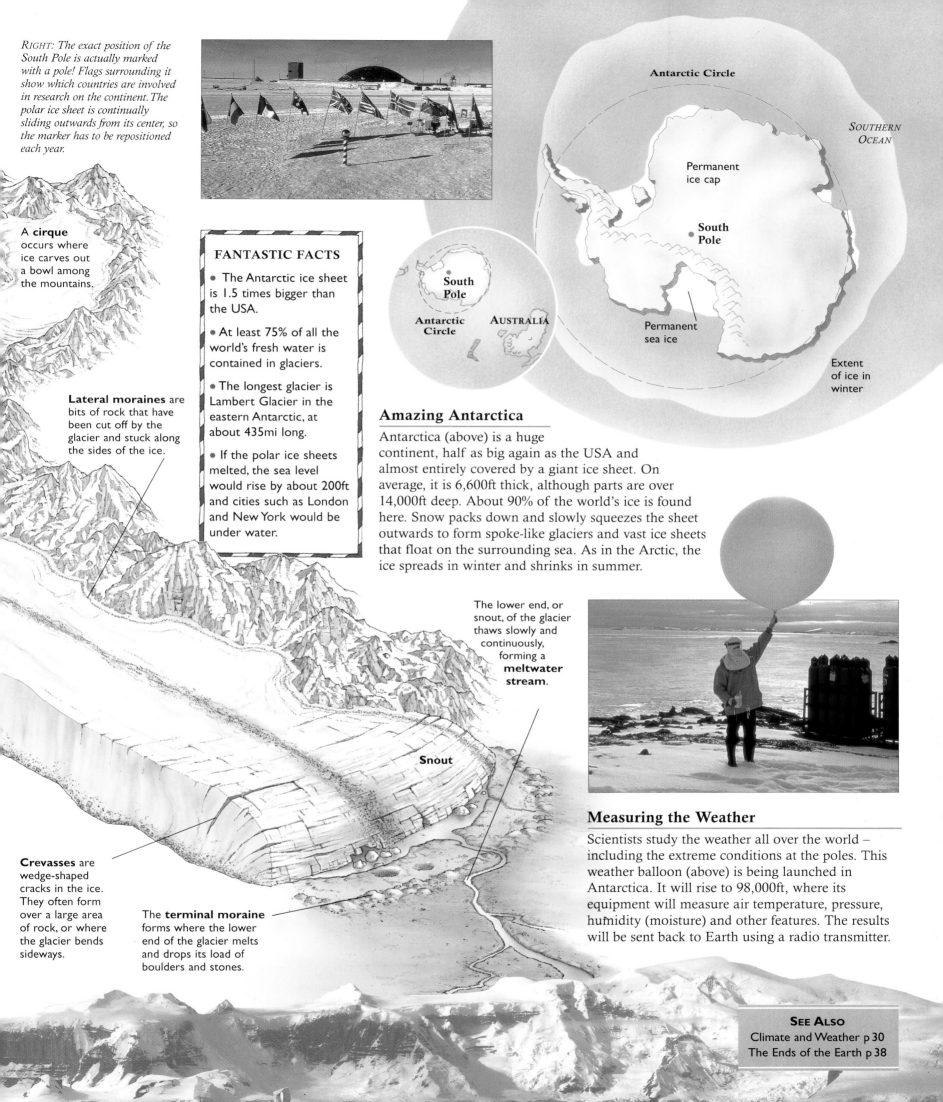

RIGHT: The exact position of the South Pole is actually marked with a pole! Flags surrounding it show which countries are involved in research on the continent. The polar ice sheet is continually sliding outwards from its center, so the marker has to be repositioned each year.

Antarctic Circle

SOUTHERN OCEAN

Permanent ice cap

South Pole

Permanent sea ice

Extent of ice in winter

South Pole

Antarctic Circle   **AUSTRALIA**

A **cirque** occurs where ice carves out a bowl among the mountains.

FANTASTIC FACTS

• The Antarctic ice sheet is 1.5 times bigger than the USA.

• At least 75% of all the world's fresh water is contained in glaciers.

• The longest glacier is Lambert Glacier in the eastern Antarctic, at about 435mi long.

• If the polar ice sheets melted, the sea level would rise by about 200ft and cities such as London and New York would be under water.

Lateral moraines are bits of rock that have been cut off by the glacier and stuck along the sides of the ice.

Amazing Antarctica

Antarctica (above) is a huge continent, half as big again as the USA and almost entirely covered by a giant ice sheet. On average, it is 6,600ft thick, although parts are over 14,000ft deep. About 90% of the world's ice is found here. Snow packs down and slowly squeezes the sheet outwards to form spoke-like glaciers and vast ice sheets that float on the surrounding sea. As in the Arctic, the ice spreads in winter and shrinks in summer.

The lower end, or snout, of the glacier thaws slowly and continuously, forming a **meltwater stream**.

Snout

Crevasses are wedge-shaped cracks in the ice. They often form over a large area of rock, or where the glacier bends sideways.

The **terminal moraine** forms where the lower end of the glacier melts and drops its load of boulders and stones.

Measuring the Weather

Scientists study the weather all over the world – including the extreme conditions at the poles. This weather balloon (above) is being launched in Antarctica. It will rise to 98,000ft, where its equipment will measure air temperature, pressure, humidity (moisture) and other features. The results will be sent back to Earth using a radio transmitter.

SEE ALSO
Climate and Weather p 30
The Ends of the Earth p 38

RIVERS AND VALLEYS

Every day, billions of raindrops fall and gather in streams and brooks. These minor waterways join rivers that cut across the countryside, finally flowing into the sea. As they wind their way, rivers wear grooves called valleys into the Earth's surface. Valleys are also formed by glaciers and by movements of the land. Rivers not only help shape the land, they provide us with water, transport and a cheap supply of energy.

From the Mountain to the Sea

Most rivers begin high up in mountains. Sometimes water from porous or spongy rocks oozes out of the hillside, as a spring. At first the flow is fast on the steep slopes, especially when the river is swollen with floodwaters from melting snow and ice. But it slows on the foothills and gently drifts through the plains. As the Earth's movements lift and tilt the land, the river makes new courses as part of the ever-changing landscape.

On the flatter lowlands, the current slows and the river may become wider and shallower. Plants, fish and other wildlife thrive. More streams join, increasing the river's size as it curves, or meanders, through the plain.

BELOW: Hydroelectric power is a clean form of energy and is a good way of harnessing the Earth's natural resources.

The river rushes down the mountain, carrying boulders that wear deep channels in its bed.

A dam across the narrow valley holds back the water. Some water is piped away to irrigate lowland fields. The rest is used to make hydroelectricity.

ABOVE: The spectacular Niagara Falls lie on the US-Canadian border. There are two falls – the Horseshoe Falls shown here are named after their curved shape.

Rivers create a barrier for travellers, so bridges and tunnels are used to cross them.

Cantilever bridge

Arched bridge

ABOVE: Arched bridges date back to Roman times. Suspension bridges are ideal for crossing wide spans.

Suspension bridge

The Power of Rivers

Dams are used to create hydroelectricity – electrical power made from running water. The water flows through turbines inside the dam, spinning the turbine's blades to turn generators and produce electricity. Hilly countries with high rainfall, such as Norway and Zaire, make more than 90% of their electricity this way.

Towns and cities are often built on rivers. The river provides fresh water, a means of transport for goods and people, plus food such as fish and other animals. It is also used for getting rid of waste.

The point at which two rivers join is called the confluence.

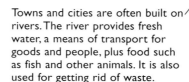

Canyons, such as the Grand Canyon in the USA, form when fast-flowing rivers cut V-shaped valleys into the rock. Small streams and tributaries wear away the sides.

U-shaped valleys are left behind when a glacier or slow-moving "ice river" melts. The fjords in Norway are deep valleys that were once gouged out by glaciers.

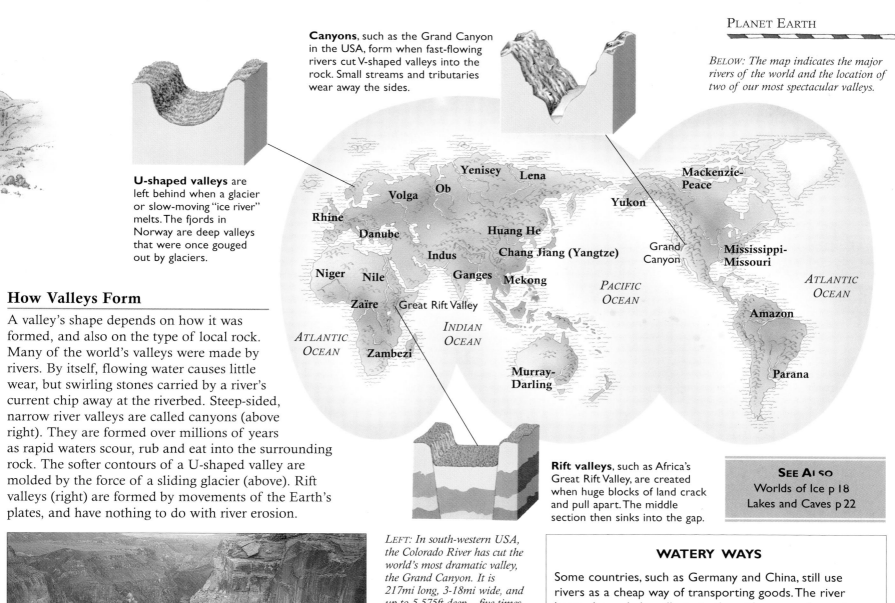

Yenisey   Lena

Volga   Ob

Mackenzie-Peace

Yukon

Rhine

Huang He

Danube

Chang Jiang (Yangtze)

Grand Canyon

Mississippi-Missouri

Indus

ATLANTIC OCEAN

Niger   Nile   Ganges   Mekong

PACIFIC OCEAN

Zaïre   Great Rift Valley

ATLANTIC OCEAN

INDIAN OCEAN

Amazon

Zambezi

Murray-Darling

Parana

How Valleys Form

A valley's shape depends on how it was formed, and also on the type of local rock. Many of the world's valleys were made by rivers. By itself, flowing water causes little wear, but swirling stones carried by a river's current chip away at the riverbed. Steep-sided, narrow river valleys are called canyons (above right). They are formed over millions of years as rapid waters scour, rub and eat into the surrounding rock. The softer contours of a U-shaped valley are molded by the force of a sliding glacier (above). Rift valleys (right) are formed by movements of the Earth's plates, and have nothing to do with river erosion.

Rift valleys, such as Africa's Great Rift Valley, are created when huge blocks of land crack and pull apart. The middle section then sinks into the gap.

> **SEE ALSO**
> Worlds of Ice p 18
> Lakes and Caves p 22

LEFT: In south-western USA, the Colorado River has cut the world's most dramatic valley, the Grand Canyon. It is 217mi long, 3-18mi wide, and up to 5,575ft deep – five times the height of the Empire State Building in New York. Rocks at the bottom of the valley are almost 1,000 million years old.

WATERY WAYS

Some countries, such as Germany and China, still use rivers as a cheap way of transporting goods. The river boats shown below illustrate the wide range of vessels that are used – some have changed little in thousands of years. Unfortunately, as cities and industries grow, some rivers become polluted and ridden with disease. Detroit River in the USA became so thick with chemicals it actually caught fire! New laws and regulations are being introduced to clean up dirty rivers.

Chinese sampan

South American reed boat

North American leather canoe

German river barge

Near the sea, a river may form a delta, splitting up among banks of sand, mud and silt. The water is partly salty, as the sea washes in at high tide.

In a long river, water takes up to a month to flow from the start, or source, to the river's end – the mouth, or estuary. Some estuaries are big ports and industrial centers, while others are teeming with wildlife.

LAKES AND CAVES

Lakes and caves have been important to people for millions of years. Fossil bones and stone tools of early humans, found in Africa, show that caves were our ancestors' first homes. As people began to build dwellings, they founded their settlements on lakeshores, often where a river joined a lake, for plentiful supplies of water and fish. Many of these lakeside villages have grown into modern cities.

BELOW: The map shows the world's great lakes. The largest, Lake Superior, is one of five lakes in North America, know collectively as the Great Lakes.

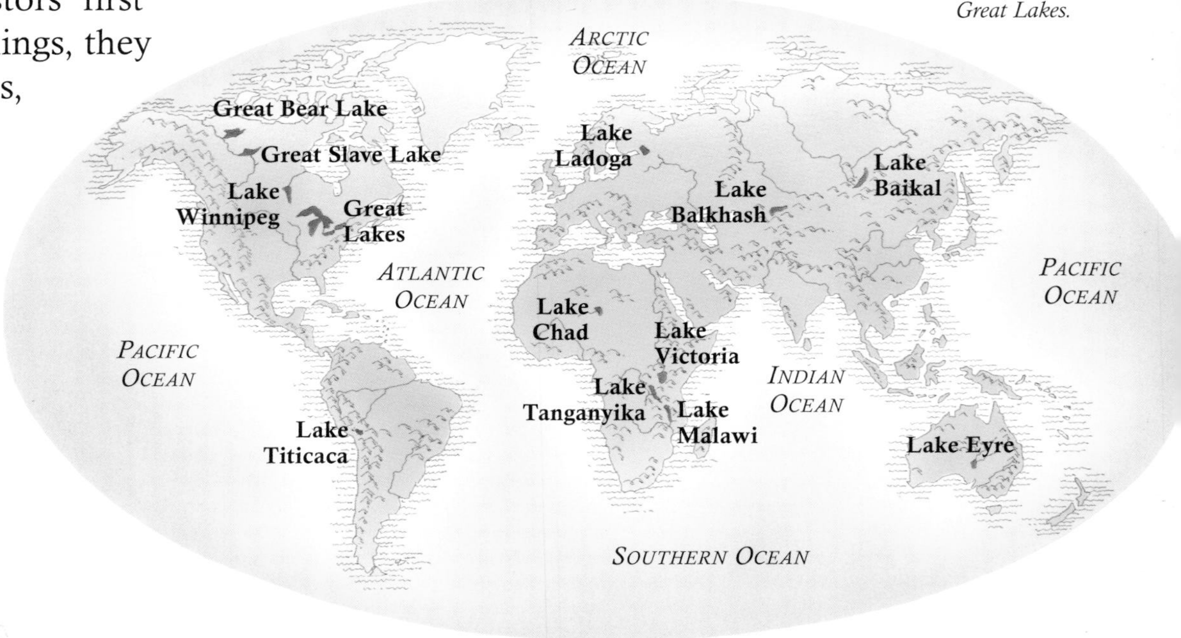

On the map: Great Bear Lake, Great Slave Lake, Lake Winnipeg, Great Lakes, Lake Ladoga, Lake Balkhash, Lake Baikal, Lake Chad, Lake Victoria, Lake Tanganyika, Lake Malawi, Lake Titicaca, Lake Eyre. ARCTIC OCEAN, ATLANTIC OCEAN, PACIFIC OCEAN, PACIFIC OCEAN, INDIAN OCEAN, SOUTHERN OCEAN.

Looking at Lakes

What a lake is like depends on how the hollow in the land was formed, and where the water comes from. Most big lakes are fed and drained by rivers. In still, or standing, lakes the flow of water is caused by rain or groundwater soaking through the rocks below. Water moves around the lake due to wind and warming by the Sun.

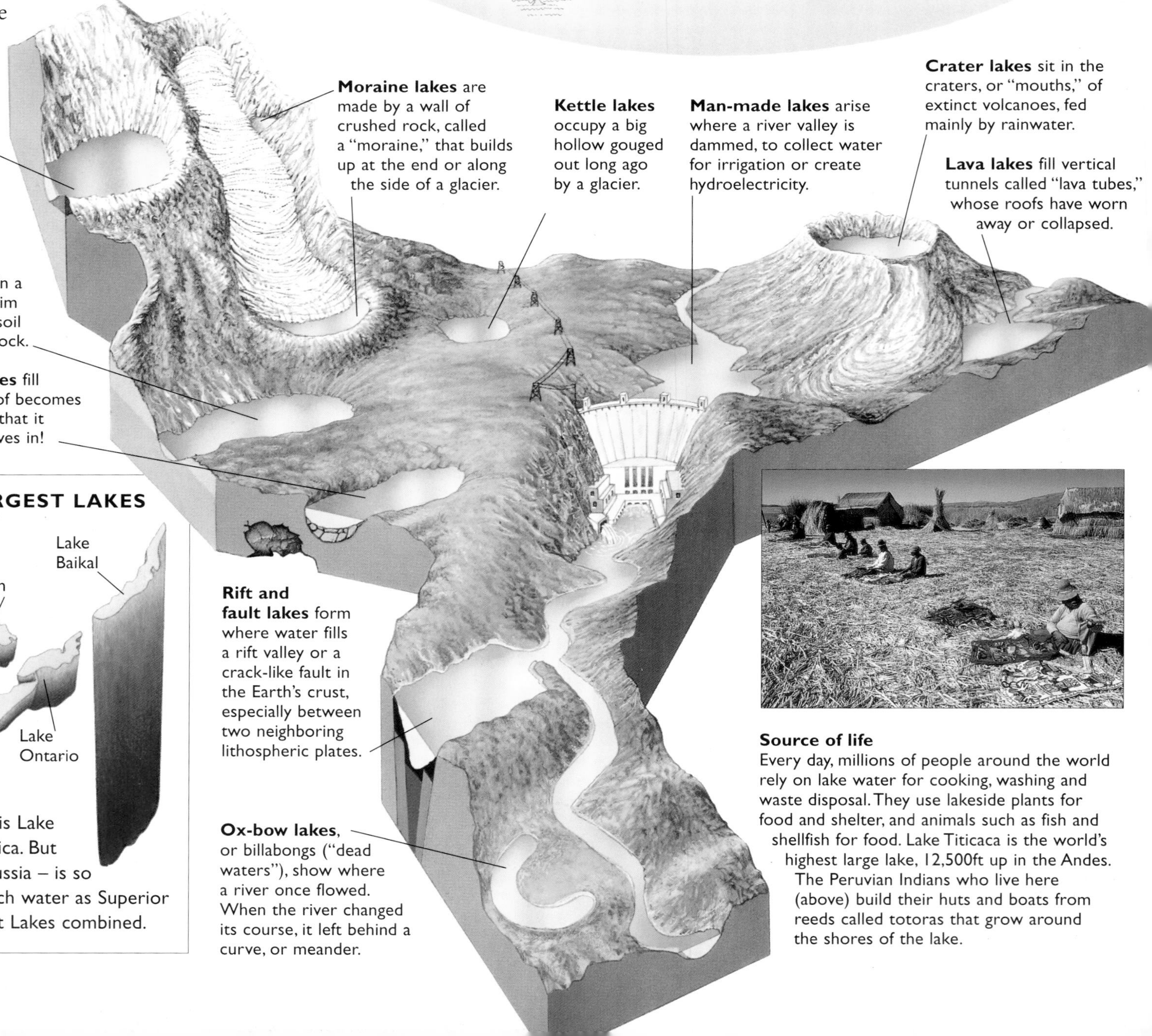

Cirque lakes, or tarns, form in the head of a valley, where ice gouges out a circular bowl and piles up a rocky wall, then melts.

Deflation lakes lie in a hollow formed by a rim of loose, windblown soil and other pieces of rock.

Collapsed-cave lakes fill caverns when the roof becomes so eroded and weak that it collapses – that is, caves in!

Moraine lakes are made by a wall of crushed rock, called a "moraine," that builds up at the end or along the side of a glacier.

Kettle lakes occupy a big hollow gouged out long ago by a glacier.

Man-made lakes arise where a river valley is dammed, to collect water for irrigation or create hydroelectricity.

Crater lakes sit in the craters, or "mouths," of extinct volcanoes, fed mainly by rainwater.

Lava lakes fill vertical tunnels called "lava tubes," whose roofs have worn away or collapsed.

THE WORLD'S LARGEST LAKES

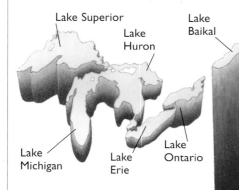

Lake Superior, Lake Huron, Lake Baikal, Lake Michigan, Lake Erie, Lake Ontario

The largest lake by area is Lake Superior, in North America. But Baikal – a fault lake in Russia – is so deep that it holds as much water as Superior and the other four Great Lakes combined.

Rift and fault lakes form where water fills a rift valley or a crack-like fault in the Earth's crust, especially between two neighboring lithospheric plates.

Ox-bow lakes, or billabongs ("dead waters"), show where a river once flowed. When the river changed its course, it left behind a curve, or meander.

Source of life

Every day, millions of people around the world rely on lake water for cooking, washing and waste disposal. They use lakeside plants for food and shelter, and animals such as fish and shellfish for food. Lake Titicaca is the world's highest large lake, 12,500ft up in the Andes. The Peruvian Indians who live here (above) build their huts and boats from reeds called totoras that grow around the shores of the lake.

ABOVE: Dominica Cave, in Slovakia, displays beautiful rock formations called stalagmites (that rise from the ground) and stalactites (that hang from the roof). In constant conditions, these features grow about half an inch every five years. Another Slovakian cave boasts the world's tallest stalagmite, 105ft high. Stalactites are more fragile – the biggest known, in the Janelano Grotto in Brazil, is 40ft long.

Crystal Icicles

Water trickling through the roof of a cave contains traces of calcium carbonate minerals (calcite or aragonite), dissolved from the rocks above. As the water dries, it leaves behind these minerals which slowly build up to form stalactites – long, thin tubes of sparkling rock crystals.

Stalactite

SEE ALSO
Wetland Wildlife p 48
The First People p 66

A **pot hole** is a dry hole, showing where a stream or river disappeared underground.

A **chimney** is a vertical passage worn away by a tumbling waterfall.

A **dry gallery** is a horizontal passage, dissolved and worn away by a stream which has since changed its course.

FANTASTIC FACTS

• Between them, the Great Lakes of North America and Baikal hold about two-fifths of all the world's surface water.

• Only 0.03% of the planet's water collects in lakes and rivers.

• The largest single cave, Sarawak Chamber in South East Asia, could house 15 soccer fields.

• Most animals that live in caves, such as newts, fish, crayfish, crickets and beetles, are white as well as blind. This is because colors and sight are unnecessary in the dark.

A stream or small river enters the cave system through a **swallow hole**, or sink hole.

A **siphon,** or sump, is a place where the cave roof dips below the current water level.

A **chamber,** or cavern, is wider and higher than a gallery, and may have terraces and balconies along its sides.

The stream or river emerges back into the open air at its **resurgence**, which may be many miles from its swallow hole.

If a stalactite growing down meets and joins an upcoming stalagmite, the result is called a **column**.

A **flooded gallery** may be occupied by the stream which formed it, or by a new stream following a dry period.

RIGHT: Pot-holing is a popular activity. But when people explore caves, they change the motion and make-up of the air, which can be damaging. Some caves have limited access to protect the fragile environment.

Water drips have a high mineral content.

A Hidden World

A cave system such as the one above forms in limestone rock over thousands of years, as rainwater – a weak natural acid – gradually dissolves the calcium carbonate minerals in the rock. Water trickles down and along any crevices in the rock, breaking down the minerals and slowly enlarging narrow cracks into wider holes and tunnels. Streams and rivers start to flow through the undergound caverns and passageways, wearing away more rock, and beautiful features such as stalagmites and stalactites form. As water levels rise and fall, and rivers change their course, the caves may be left dry or flooded for long periods of time.

Stalagmite

Towers of Crystal

Stalagmites form as drops of water splash on to the cave floor. The sudden rise in pressure within the drop causes minerals in the water to crystallize out. Most stalagmites are cone-shaped but, depending on how the water drips, other shapes may form, such as smooth bowls or curtains.

OCEANS AND SEAS

ABOVE: The Pacific Ocean makes up half of the world's watery area. All the Earth's lands – 148 million km² – would fit in the Pacific with room to spare.

BELOW: The map shows the major ridges and trenches beneath the world's oceans.

About 97% of the Earth's water is found in oceans and seas. The three main oceans are the Pacific, Atlantic and Indian Oceans. Their southern parts join together to form the Southern or Antarctic Ocean, with the Arctic Ocean in the north. Seas are smaller than oceans, and more enclosed by land. Under most seas and oceans lie flat sea beds called abyssal plains. They are 16,400-19,700ft below the waves, and ooze with sand, silt and mud.

Down in the depths
This diagram shows the depth of the Marianas Trench in the north-west Pacific. It is the world's lowest point, 35,798ft below sea level. Mount Everest, turned upside-down, would fit in with 6,500ft to spare. The first people to descend here were Jacques Picard and Donald Walsh in the bathyscaphe ("deep ship") *Trieste*, in 1960.

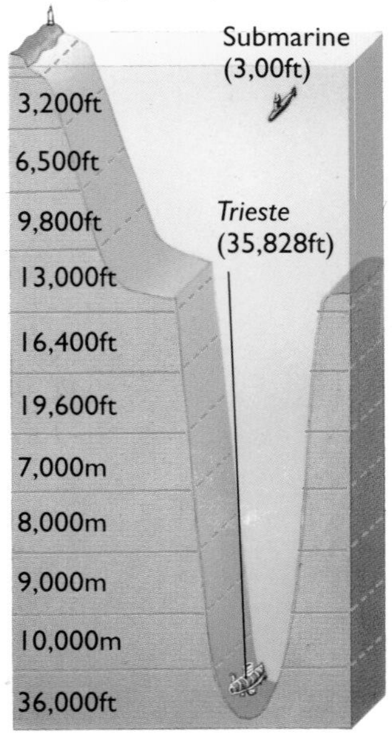

Empire State Building (1,250ft)
Submarine (3,00ft)
3,200ft
6,500ft
9,800ft
13,000ft
16,400ft
19,600ft
7,000m
8,000m
9,000m
10,000m
36,000ft
Trieste (35,828ft)

LEFT: Ordinary submarines only go down about 2,300-2,950ft below the surface. Manned submersibles like Deep-Star 4,000, *designed to reach depths of 4,000ft, have thick hulls to withstand the high water pressure.*

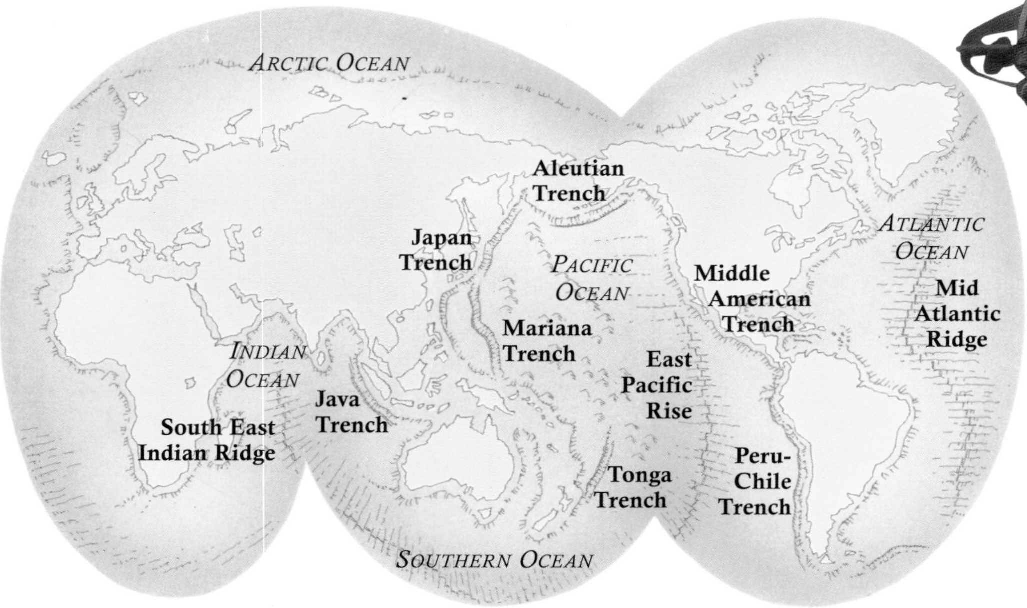

ARCTIC OCEAN
Aleutian Trench
Japan Trench
PACIFIC OCEAN
Middle American Trench
ATLANTIC OCEAN
Mid Atlantic Ridge
Mariana Trench
East Pacific Rise
INDIAN OCEAN
Java Trench
South East Indian Ridge
Tonga Trench
Peru-Chile Trench
SOUTHERN OCEAN

Exploring the Deep

The ocean depths are the last great unexplored regions on Earth. Their hills and valleys have been mapped by ship's sonar, a type of sound-radar. Sonar beams high-pitched sound waves through the water, to bounce off the bottom as echoes which are detected and analyzed. Only a tiny fraction of this pitch-black, cold habitat has been seen by human eyes. Most exploration today, such as searching for shipwrecks, or observing the weird wildlife, is by remote-controlled robot submersibles with video cameras and other monitoring equipment.

The Undersea World

Take the water out of the oceans, and you would see a land of rocky slopes, sandy hollows, flat muddy plains, sheer cliffs, towering mountains and steep plunging canyons. The huge lithospheric plates that make up the Earth's surface move very slowly to change the face of the sea bed, as well as that of the land. The coastlines are not the main edges of the continents – the true edges are the continental slopes that plunge from shallow waters to the ocean floor.

Around the coast the sea is ususally less than 650ft deep, as the land slopes gently into the **continental shelf.**

The **continental slope** lies at the end of the continental shelf. Here, the land drops steeply down to the flat abyssal plains.

A **mid-oceanic ridge** forms where molten rocks well up through a gigantic crack and add to the edges of two plates.

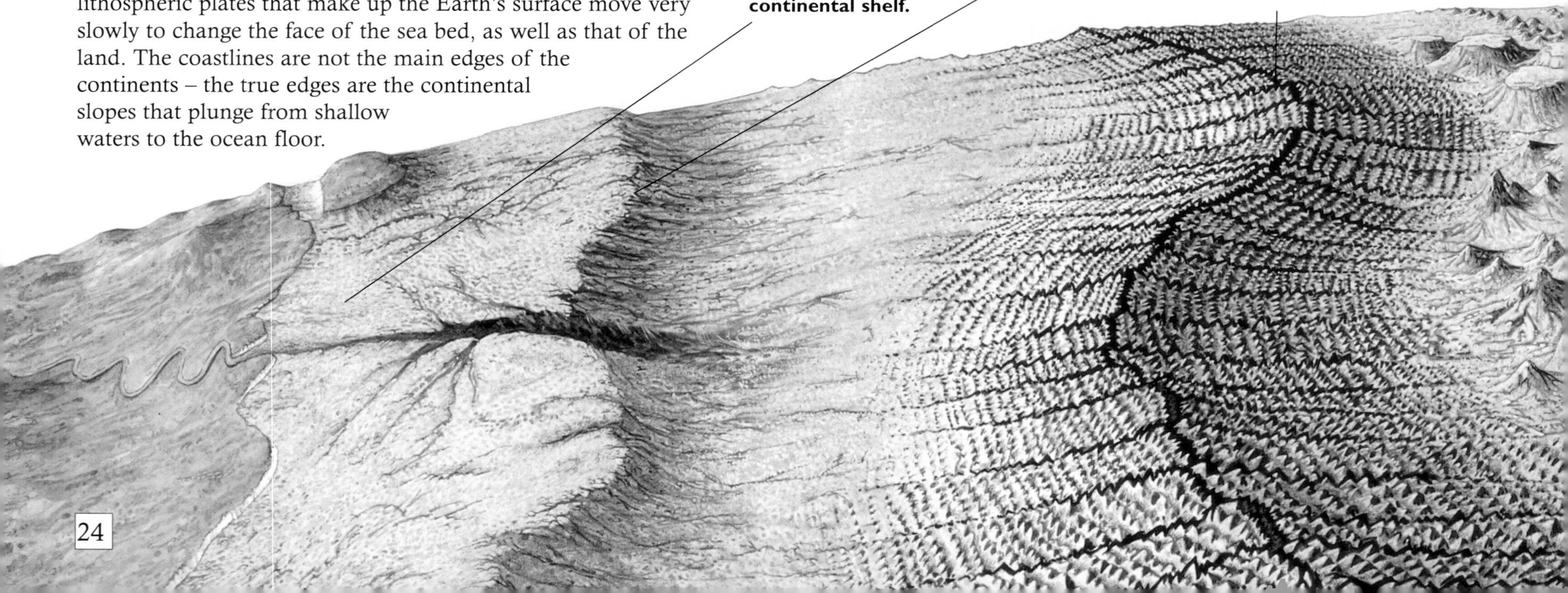

The **cliff base** is worn away by the constant beating of the waves. Hanging rock above finally collapses and the sea breaks up the boulders.

ABOVE: A wave crashes into a cave in the coastline, then bursts through a blowhole in the rocks above.

Headland

Cliff

Bay

Beach

Salt marsh

Coastal defence

Groyne

Tidal estuary

Blowhole

Cave **Arch** **Stack**

Coastal dunes

Spit

Headlands and peninsulars are made of the toughest coastal rocks. Softer rocks are eroded to form bays.

Groynes and sea walls are built to stop sand being swept away.

Blowholes are created where waves smash through a crack in the rock.

Arches are carved by the power of the waves. When the top of an arch collapses, it leaves behind a single **stack**.

Shaping the Shoreline

Waves never stop pounding the sea shore. They vary from small ripples to gigantic crashing breakers. Over centuries, they wear away even the hardest rocks, such as granite. Yet they also build up formations such as mud flats, sand bars and single spits. The many different features of a shoreline (right) are shaped by natural forces such as waves, winds, tides and water currents.

Spits, bars and banks form in sheltered areas, when water leaves behind sand, silt and mud.

Sucking up the sea
In warmer parts of the world, in thundery weather, winds may start to spin around like a top. This forms a waterspout – a swirling column of air and water that links thunder-type cumulonimbus clouds with high-splashing spray from the sea below. Similar to a tornado on land, it sucks sea water up into the clouds. The spout can be 1,640ft tall and last up to one hour as it surges across the surface of the ocean.

Volcanoes under the sea erupt regularly, building mountains, or **seamounts**, on the sea bed. Their peaks may rise above the surface to form small islands.

Oceans in Peril

Despite strict safety measures and shipping laws, environmental accidents still happen at sea. They may be oil spills, as in 1996 when the supertanker *Sea Empress* spewed 70,000 tons of crude oil off Milford Haven, south-west Wales (below). It is also disastrous when chemicals such as mercury are spilled into the sea, or undersea pipelines burst.

FANTASTIC FACTS

• Only just over 1% of the world's ocean area is more than 20,000ft deep.

• The largest accurately measured wave, recorded during a Pacific hurricane, was 112ft high – as tall as a ten-storey building.

• The water in the oceans is permanently moving round the globe, flowing in vast currents, like rivers in the sea. Ocean currents may be 50mi wide and flow up to 4mi/h.

• In 1985 the robot submersible *Argo* found the wreck of the huge ocean liner *Titanic*, which sank in 1912.

As the thin oceanic crust of one lithospheric plate slides under the thick continental crust of the next plate, a **deep-sea trench** is formed.

A row of undersea volcanoes along the edge of a lithospheric plate forms an island arc, or **archipelago**.

SEE ALSO
Polluting Our Planet p 34
Life Beneath the Waves p 52

DESERTS HOT AND COLD

All deserts are dry – in an average year, they get less than 10in of rain, hail, dew and other forms of moisture. Many deserts are scorching hot, with an average temperature of 80°F, but others are bitterly cold at less than 35°F. Some are both hot and cold, depending on the time of day or the season. Only one-third of the world's desert areas are sandy, the rest are rocky or stony, or covered with ice.

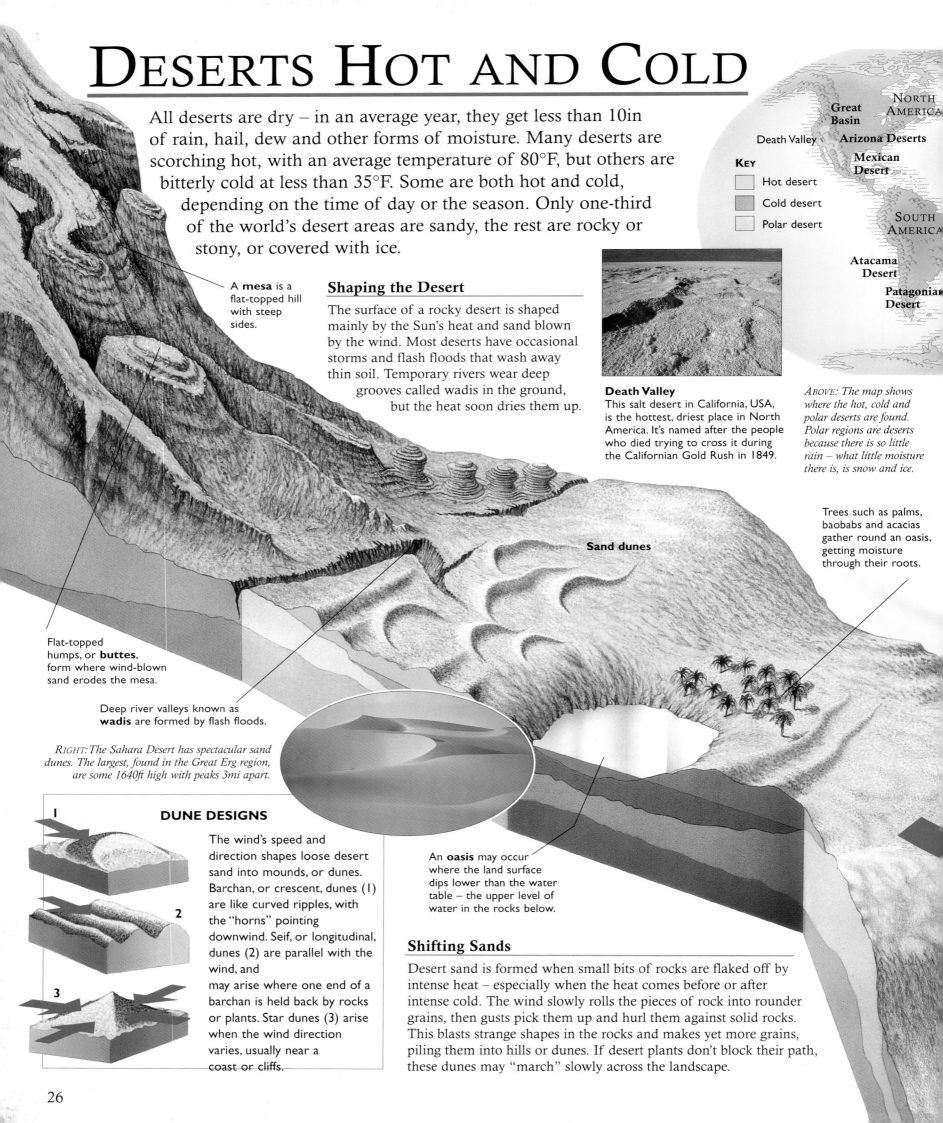

A **mesa** is a flat-topped hill with steep sides.

KEY
- Hot desert
- Cold desert
- Polar desert

NORTH AMERICA
Great Basin
Death Valley
Arizona Deserts
Mexican Desert
SOUTH AMERICA
Atacama Desert
Patagonian Desert

Shaping the Desert

The surface of a rocky desert is shaped mainly by the Sun's heat and sand blown by the wind. Most deserts have occasional storms and flash floods that wash away thin soil. Temporary rivers wear deep grooves called wadis in the ground, but the heat soon dries them up.

Death Valley
This salt desert in California, USA, is the hottest, driest place in North America. It's named after the people who died trying to cross it during the Californian Gold Rush in 1849.

ABOVE: The map shows where the hot, cold and polar deserts are found. Polar regions are deserts because there is so little rain – what little moisture there is, is snow and ice.

Sand dunes

Trees such as palms, baobabs and acacias gather round an oasis, getting moisture through their roots.

Flat-topped humps, or **buttes**, form where wind-blown sand erodes the mesa.

Deep river valleys known as **wadis** are formed by flash floods.

RIGHT: The Sahara Desert has spectacular sand dunes. The largest, found in the Great Erg region, are some 1640ft high with peaks 3mi apart.

DUNE DESIGNS

The wind's speed and direction shapes loose desert sand into mounds, or dunes. Barchan, or crescent, dunes (1) are like curved ripples, with the "horns" pointing downwind. Seif, or longitudinal, dunes (2) are parallel with the wind, and may arise where one end of a barchan is held back by rocks or plants. Star dunes (3) arise when the wind direction varies, usually near a coast or cliffs.

An **oasis** may occur where the land surface dips lower than the water table – the upper level of water in the rocks below.

Shifting Sands

Desert sand is formed when small bits of rocks are flaked off by intense heat – especially when the heat comes before or after intense cold. The wind slowly rolls the pieces of rock into rounder grains, then gusts pick them up and hurl them against solid rocks. This blasts strange shapes in the rocks and makes yet more grains, piling them into hills or dunes. If desert plants don't block their path, these dunes may "march" slowly across the landscape.

ARCTIC REGIONS

ASIA

EUROPE

Turkestan
Desert

Gobi Desert

Takla
Makan Desert

Sahara Desert

Arabian
Desert

Indian
Desert

AFRICA

AUSTRALIA

Namib
Desert

Kalahari
Desert

Australian
Deserts

ANTARCTICA

Pillars in the sand
Australia is, on average, the driest continent. These tall pinnacles of limestone rock (left) that rise out of the sandy desert in western Australia are shaped mainly by the sand-blasting effect of the wind.

SEE ALSO
Climate and Weather p 30
Desert Survival p 50

Sand sculptures
In desert lands, sand grains tossed by storms rub rocks into amazing shapes, such as pillars, arches, domes and tabletops. If they cut into the soft sides of a tall rock, leaving the harder rock on top, a strange mushroom-type form called a zeugen is created (see left).

Hard rock at the top of a zeugen is called the cap.

Zeugen

Desert winds can reach up to 125mi/h.

Strong winds lash at the rock, carrying sand that eats away, or erodes, the softer, lower parts.

FANTASTIC FACTS

● The driest place on Earth is a region of Antarctica where it hasn't rained for 2 million years!

● The Gobi Desert has the widest temperature range, from 120°F in the day to -40°F at night.

● About 5,000 years ago parts of the Sahara were moist and green. Ancient art and bones show that people, elephants and rhinos once lived there.

Foggy wilderness
The Namib is a foggy desert along the shores of south-west Africa, 995mi long yet mostly less than 60mi wide. The rainfall is only 1in a year, but moist Atlantic air brings fog which turns to dew, so animals such as elephants and lions can survive there.

The Growing Desert

Desert-type landscapes are not only produced by nature, but also by humans. In dry places, too many crops use up all the goodness in the thin soil, while logging or farm animals remove the natural vegetation that protects the surface. As a result, soil turns to dry dust and blows away – this is called desertification. In the past few centuries the south-west of the Sahara has spread by up to 620mi into the dry Sahel region, because of this damaging process.

Salt pans are flat areas of salty minerals, mainly rock salt. They form when rain washes salt out of the rocks, then dries, leaving layers of gleaming salt crystals on the ground.

At the edge of the desert, desert winds drive the sand and dusty soil over farmland.

Zeugens form as wind sweeps over the desert.

The shifting sandscape has turned this settlement into a desert ghost town.

Zeugens

Wind direction

WONDERS OF THE WORLD

The Earth's surface is constantly changing, thanks to the power of natural forces such as plate movements and other factors like wind and rain. Sometimes, the elements are destructive, for example earthquakes and storms can cause enormous damage. But the forces of nature also create breathtaking beauty and awesome scenery, from huge sculpted rocks to high waterfalls and spectacular glowing skies.

Grand Canyon
The Colorado River eroded this fantastic gorge in Arizona, USA, millions of years ago. It is 217mi long, 3-18mi wide and up to 5,575ft deep. The rocks at the bottom of the valley are about 1,000 million years old.

ABOVE: In Utah, USA, the limestone cliffs of Bryce Canyon have been worn into pinnacles, towers, bowls and other fascinating geometric shapes called hoodoos.

Towering Cascade

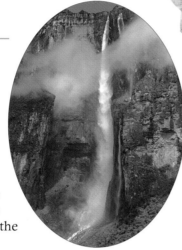

The world's tallest falls are the Angel Falls, which lie on the River Churún in Venezuela, South America (right). A cascade of water tumbles down a massive main drop of 3,210ft – over three times the height of the Eiffel Tower! The falls were named after the American adventurere Jimmy Angel who came across them in 1935 while flying over the region prospecting for gold.

Touched by the Elements

Monument Valley (below) is a spectacular area of Arizona and Utah, USA, where tall red sandstone towers, arches, mesas, buttes and other rock formations, stand above the sandy plain. These rocky features have been eroded by wind, sand and rain throughout their history. Like many places of great beauty, the valley is a protected region. It is also part of the Native American Navajo Reserve.

Bryce Canyon

Grand Canyon

Barringer Crater

Mammoth Caves

Mammoth Caves
Under Kentucky, USA, lies the world's biggest and most amazing system of limestone caves and tunnels – at least 350mi long on five separate levels, with more still waiting to be explored.

Angel Falls

Tepuís

Barringer Crater
About 27,000 years ago, a huge meteorite (lump of rock) from outer space smashed into the Earth and made this vast hole near Winslow, in Arizona. Also called the Meteor Crater, it's a massive 4,150ft across and 590ft deep, the largest such crater in the world.

Flat-topped tepuis
These beautiful table-top mountains, called tepuís by the local Indians, rise high above the steamy rainforests of north eastern South America.

Sugarloaf Mountain
This thin, 1,295ft-tall mountain is a famous landmark near the city of Rio de Janeiro, in Brazil. It has a rounded top and gets its name from the mould once used to shape blocks of sugar.

Sugarloaf Mountain

Torres del Paine
In southern Chile, these rocky spires of pink granite tipped with black slate rise to a towering height of 8,500ft. They were shaped by glaciers and movements in the Earth's crust.

Torres del Paine mountains

High Lights

The Earth is surrounded by an invisible force called a magnetic field. When the Sun's rays pass through the strongest parts of this magnetic field, near the poles, they create fantastic displays of colored lights, 100-300km up in the night sky. These are known as the Northern and Southern Lights.

SEE ALSO
Mountain Building p16
Deserts Hot and Cold p26

LEFT: The Northern Lights, or Aurora Borealis, light up the night sky with stunning splashes of color. The Southern Lights are also called the Aurora Australis.

FANTASTIC FACTS

• As the Grand Canyon formed, over 2 million million cubic metres of rock were swept away, but no one knows where it all ended up.

• The world's highest geyser was New Zealand's Waimangu, which shot water over 1,475ft into the air. Its last spurt happened in 1917, killing four people.

• One Antarctic iceberg was found to be bigger than Belgium! It took four years to thaw.

Giant's Causeway
This geometric rock formation on Ireland's north coast was created when volcanic lava cooled quickly, forming hundreds of six-sided columns, 12-20in across.

Giant's Causeway

Externsteine

Externsteine
Held sacred in ancient times, these strange limestone formations in Germany later became a Christian site, and a chapel was cut into the rock.

The Himalayas
The world's greatest mountain range is the Himalayas in central Asia. Over 1,500mi long and up to 250mi wide, it contains the world's tallest mountain – Everest – plus the next 27 tallest peaks .

Mount Fuji
Japan's tallest natural feature is an almost cone-shaped volcano called Mount Fuji. Rising 12,390ft high, it last erupted in 1707.

Mount Fuji

Chang Jiang Gorges

Himalayas

Sahara Desert
The largest expanse of desert on Earth almost fills the whole of North Africa. It is up to 1,360mi from north to south and 3,230mi from east to west.

Chang Jiang Gorges
Formed by the world's third-longest river – the Chang Jiang (Yangtze) – three spectacular, steep-sided gorges run for a total of 120mi through central China.

ABOVE: The Great Barrier Reef is the world's biggest animal-made feature, at over 1,250mi long. It was built over millions of years from the tiny stone cups of anemone-like coral polyps. The reef is home to many sea creatures and plants, and is a giant marine reserve.

Victoria Falls
On the Zambesi River, at the Zambia-Zimbabwe border, these massive waterfalls are 360ft high and 5,480ft wide.

Victoria Falls

Wave rocks
Blasted smooth by waves, wind and rain, various weird rock formations, shaped like waves, are found along the coasts of Western and South Australia.

Great Barrier Reef

Ayers Rock

Wave rocks

Geysers

Table Mountain
This famous mountain south of Cape Town, South Africa, rises 3,550ft above sea level. It is sometimes covered in a layer of mist, nicknamed "the tablecloth."

Table Mountain

BELOW: Uluru, or Ayers Rock, is the planet's biggest and most famous isolated rock. It is 1.5mi long and towers 1,150ft above the surrounding central Australian desert. Sacred to the local Aborignes, it dramatically changes color at sunset, finally glowing deep red.

New Zealand geysers
New Zealand is famous for its beautiful, but dangerous, geysers. Fountains of superheated water and steam shoot up out of the rocks, usually reaching heights of about 325ft.

CLIMATE AND WEATHER

Weather is the name we give to hourly and daily changes in temperature, clouds, wind and rain. All our weather takes place in the atmosphere, the layer of air around the Earth. Over years and centuries, weather in a particular area tends to follow a regular pattern, which we call the climate. The temperature in a place depends on how the Earth is tilted towards the Sun, where we are in our orbit around the Sun and the position of our planet as it spins around every 24 hours. Winds and ocean currents also affect the climate.

North Pole

SUN'S RAYS

Equator

South Pole

Sub-polar regions
Here, the brief, fairly warm summers give way to long, cold winters with lots of frost and snow. The main plants are evergreen conifers.

The Power of the Sun

All weather is driven by the Sun. Its warming rays are strongest around the planet's equator, in the tropics. Here, the Sun is directly overhead and shines straight down through the Earth's atmosphere (see diagram above). At the poles, the same amount of the Sun's rays are spread over a larger area of the Earth's surface. Also, the rays must slant through a greater amount of atmosphere, which soaks up and spreads the heat. This is why it is always so cold at the poles.

Climate zones
The world's climate can be divided into several main zones, up and down the globe (see map). The zones are generally based on average temperatures, measured over days and years. Different kinds of wildlife, particularly trees, flourish in the different conditions.

Radio antennae

Temperate regions
Halfway between the tropics and poles lie the temperate lands, with warm summers and cool, occasionally cold, winters. Deciduous trees thrive.

NORTH AMERICA

Tropic of Cancer

Equator

Tropic of Capricorn

SOUTH AMERICA

FANTASTIC FACTS

• The coldest ever air temperature was -128.6°F, recorded at Vostok Base, Antarctica, in 1983.

• Scientists can work out the temperatures long ago by examining pollen grains preserved in soil, mud and ice. The pollen came from plants that only grew at certain temperatures.

• The last Ice Age ended about 10,000 years ago, and the next one will start in 23,000 years' time.

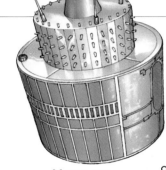

Meteo-sat

WEATHER WATCH

The scientific study of the atmosphere, weather and climate is known as meteorology. Satellites designed to detect and measure heat rays, light waves, clouds, the make-up of the atmosphere and other weather features are called meteo-sats. Some can even tell which crops are growing in a field, or measure the height of the sea's waves to within a foot. Hundreds of meteo-sats orbit the Earth, sending back information for huge computers to analyse. This helps scientists to monitor and predict, or forecast, the weather for the next few days.

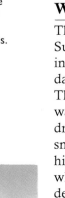

Desert regions
Dry, or arid, desert regions, and slightly wetter semi-arid lands, receive on average less than 20in of rain each year. Here, only drought-tolerant plants such as cacti survive.

KEY
- Polar and tundra
- Sub-polar
- Temperate
- Warm temperate
- Mediterranean
- Mountain
- Desert
- Tropical
- Moist tropical

Liquid rain or frozen snow falls on the land.

As it rises, the water vapour condenses, forming clouds.

Rivers carry water back to lakes and seas, and the cycle begins again.

Water evaporates from seas and lakes, rising into the air.

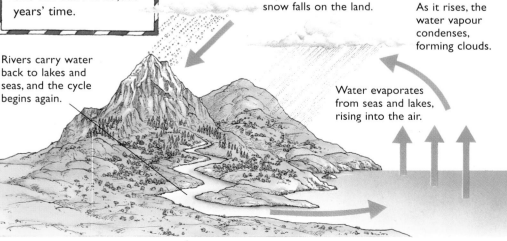

Water Works

The water cycle plays a central part in our weather. The Sun's warmth evaporates water from the seas, turning it into invisible water vapor in the air. As winds blow this damp air against hills and mountains, it rises and cools. This makes the water vapor condense back into liquid water, forming tiny droplets that gather into clouds. The droplets clump into drops that fall as rain or freeze as snow. Glaciers and rivers channel the water down the hills and across the land, back into the sea – where the whole cycle begins again. So water is not made or destroyed, it simply goes round and round. This is also why coastal areas are often cloudy and damp, while far inland we find dry areas and deserts.

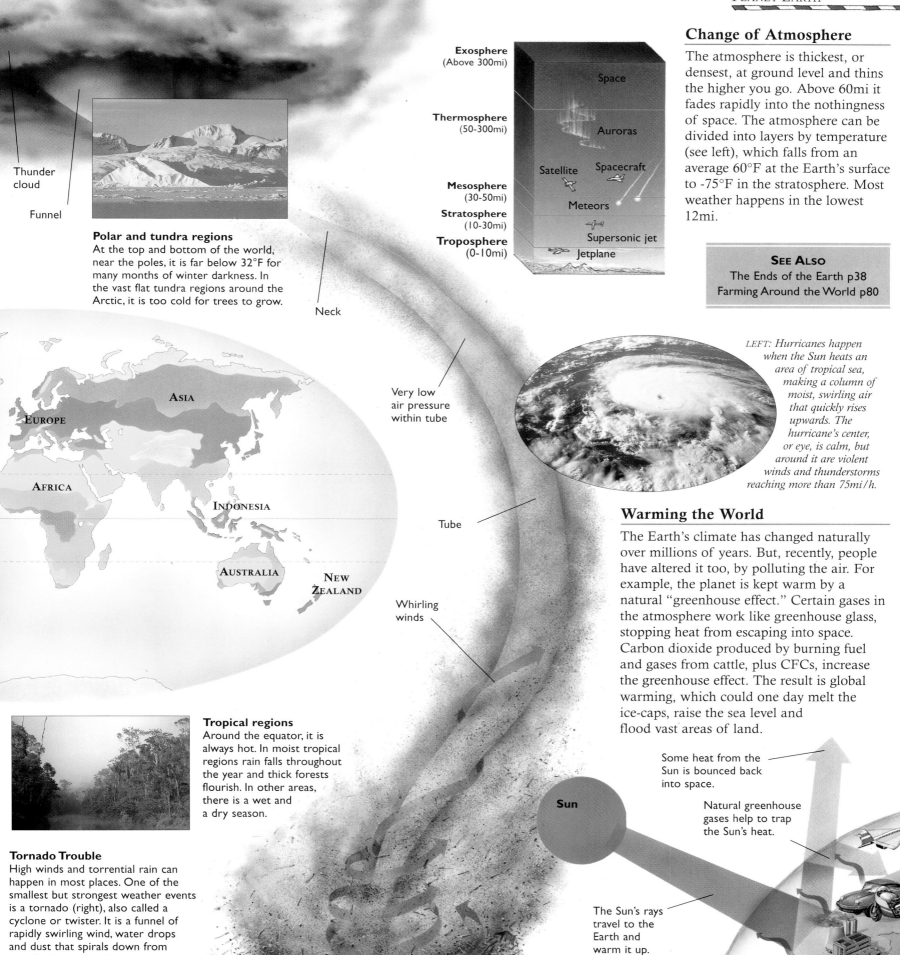

Thunder
cloud

Funnel

Polar and tundra regions
At the top and bottom of the world, near the poles, it is far below 32°F for many months of winter darkness. In the vast flat tundra regions around the Arctic, it is too cold for trees to grow.

Exosphere
(Above 300mi)

Space

Thermosphere
(50-300mi)

Auroras

Satellite

Spacecraft

Mesosphere
(30-50mi)

Stratosphere
(10-30mi)

Meteors

Troposphere
(0-10mi)

Supersonic jet

Jetplane

Change of Atmosphere

The atmosphere is thickest, or densest, at ground level and thins the higher you go. Above 60mi it fades rapidly into the nothingness of space. The atmosphere can be divided into layers by temperature (see left), which falls from an average 60°F at the Earth's surface to -75°F in the stratosphere. Most weather happens in the lowest 12mi.

SEE ALSO
The Ends of the Earth p38
Farming Around the World p80

Neck

ASIA

EUROPE

AFRICA

INDONESIA

AUSTRALIA

NEW
ZEALAND

Very low
air pressure
within tube

LEFT: Hurricanes happen when the Sun heats an area of tropical sea, making a column of moist, swirling air that quickly rises upwards. The hurricane's center, or eye, is calm, but around it are violent winds and thunderstorms reaching more than 75mi/h.

Tube

Warming the World

The Earth's climate has changed naturally over millions of years. But, recently, people have altered it too, by polluting the air. For example, the planet is kept warm by a natural "greenhouse effect." Certain gases in the atmosphere work like greenhouse glass, stopping heat from escaping into space. Carbon dioxide produced by burning fuel and gases from cattle, plus CFCs, increase the greenhouse effect. The result is global warming, which could one day melt the ice-caps, raise the sea level and flood vast areas of land.

Whirling
winds

Tropical regions
Around the equator, it is always hot. In moist tropical regions rain falls throughout the year and thick forests flourish. In other areas, there is a wet and a dry season.

Some heat from the
Sun is bounced back
into space.

Sun

Natural greenhouse
gases help to trap
the Sun's heat.

Tornado Trouble
High winds and torrential rain can happen in most places. One of the smallest but strongest weather events is a tornado (right), also called a cyclone or twister. It is a funnel of rapidly swirling wind, water drops and dust that spirals down from cumulonimbus, or thunder, clouds. The base, or "foot," may be less than 325ft across, but it travels along the ground at 6-12mi/h, picking up anything in its path. The winds are the fastest on Earth, at more than 300mi/h.

The Sun's rays
travel to the
Earth and
warm it up.

Too many greenhouse
gases trap too much
of the Sun's heat, and
the Earth overheats.

Foot

RICHES OF THE EARTH

The Earth contains minerals and raw materials that are valuable, for a variety of reasons. Hard and tough metals, like bronze and iron, are useful for making ornaments and tools. Sparkling gems are perfect for jewelry. Some rocks, such as jade and marble, can be carved into beautiful sculptures. Coal and oil are fuels that are easily burned to provide heat, light and other forms of energy. The Earth's natural resources may be precious simply because they are rare, and owning them is a sign of wealth and power.

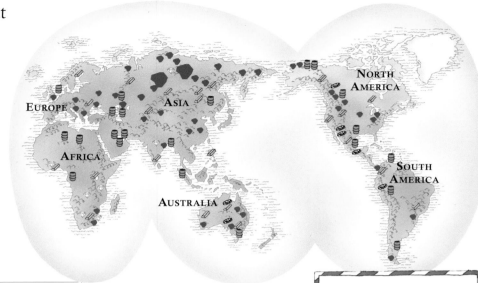

This funeral mask is made of pure gold. It was found at the site of the city of Troy, and was first thought to belong to King Agamemnon, leader of the Greek troops in the Trojan War.

Carved from rare blue jade, this head was made by the Olmec people of Central America, more than 2,000 years ago.

COSTLY BEAUTY

Rare gems and precious metals have been used for making jewelry and ornaments for thousands of years. Their value depends on the detail and skill of the design.

Made in France in 1810, this stunning jewelled plume was used as a hat pin. Its gems include diamond, turquoise, emerald, amethyst and garnet.

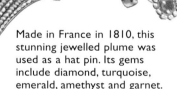

KEY

- 🪨 Coal
- 🛢 Oil
- 💍 Silver
- 📏 Gold
- 💎 Diamonds

Disappearing treasure
The map above shows where some of the world's rich resources are to be found. Scientists estimate that most major reserves of coal and oil have now been discovered. At late 20th century rates of use, coal may last 800 years, but oil and gas less than 100 years.

FANTASTIC FACTS

- Some rare metals and minerals used for high-technology equipment cost ten times more by weight than gold.

- The word bonanza comes from the town of Bonanza on the Klondike River, Canada, where gold was found in 1896, causing a gold rush.

- The biggest solid gold object is Pharaoh Tutankhamun's coffin, weighing 2,975lbs.

The Story of Coal

Coal is made from the partly rotted, preserved remains of prehistoric plants – this is why it is called a fossil fuel. On a small scale, coal has been burned for heating and metal-working for over 4,000 years. Large-scale coal-mining only began in about 1780, to fuel the fires of steam engines in the Industrial Revolution.

When plants died, they were squashed into the ground as more plants grew on top of them. They rotted and were pressed into peat.

Coal began as lush swampy forests of leafy plants, especially giant tree ferns which flourished during the Carboniferous period, 345-280 million years ago.

As time passed, the peat was buried deeper and fossilized into soft lignite, then coal and finally hard anthracite.

Black Gold

Over millions of years, the fossilized bodies of tiny sea animals and plants formed a black ooze called crude oil, or petroleum. This is pumped up through boreholes drilled by rigs into the ground or sea bed. The crude oil is heated and treated to separate it into its parts, including fuels such as gasoline and diesel, solvents, paints, plastics and hundreds of other

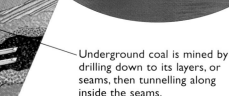

Underground coal is mined by drilling down to its layers, or seams, then tunnelling along inside the seams.

Recycling Resources

If we carry on using up the Earth's raw materials at today's fast pace, these crucial resources will soon run out. We can help by reusing things instead of throwing them away, and by using recycling banks. Paper for recycling is pulped and rolled out, ready to be made into new paper products. Glass and plastic items are cut into tiny chips before being melted down and reused, and aluminium scrap is processed to provide half the metal content of "new" cans.

Recycling bank

Roll of recycled paper

Aluminum ingots

Glass chips

Plastic chips

Newspaper

Recycled glass and plastic bottles

Aluminum cans

Supermarket basket

Energy for the Future

Nearly 90% of the world's energy comes from oil, coal and natural gas, but we are using these resources millions of times faster than they can re-form. We need to use energy sources that are renewable, instead. Most renewable sources are based on light or heat from the Sun. Others include plants grown as bio-fuels, wind, waves, and heat from deep down inside the Earth.

ABOVE: Modern "windmills" called aerogenerators turn the power of wind into electricity. But they spoil the view in these windy landscapes.

Bucket wheel excavator

A giant rotating wheel has buckets which work like huge teeth to rip up the coal from the surface.

Coal and other rocks travel along the excavator's conveyor beam to the funnel-shaped hopper, where they are loaded into huge trucks.

The bucket-wheel excavator swings around on a giant arm, gouging the ground in a series of arcs.

Out in the Open

Movements in the Earth and land erosion can bring coal seams to the surface or just below it. We get this coal by open-cast mining, with giant machines such as this bucket-wheel excavator (above). But open-casting destroys wildlife and leaves vast scars across the landscape. So, in some places, mining companies reclaim the land after mining. They start by removing the top layer of soil. Then, after they have taken the coal, they re-shape the land, re-cover it with soil, and plant trees and other vegetation.

ABOVE: The discovery of gold in a remote place often starts a gold rush, with thousands of people rushing to the site. These pioneers went to Alaska, USA, in 1900, hoping to make their fortunes.

Striking gold

Gold is hard and tough, keeps its shine, and can be melted, hammered, shaped and drawn out into fine and delicate works of art. Like most metals it is found spread through rocks, called ores. It also occurs as almost pure lumps, or nuggets. The biggest ever gold nugget was found in New South Wales, Australia, in 1872 by a prospector called Holtermann (left). It yielded 228lbs of pure gold.

SEE ALSO
Polluting Our Planet p 34
Life in the Past p 58

POLLUTING OUR PLANET

Ten thousand years ago, only about 50 million people lived on Earth. Today this number is over 100 times greater, and over three-quarters of the population live in cities. In rich countries, life is comfortable thanks to mass farming, factories, industries, and services such as transport, electricity and sewage disposal. But all these familiar things use vast amounts of our precious natural resources. They also change the balance of the environment and pollute the air, soil and water.

Unnatural Causes

In cities and industrial centres, people live close together, working to make goods from raw materials. The result, as seen below, is a dangerous mix of unnatural substances pouring into the atmosphere, rivers and soil. Most countries now have regulations to control this worrying situation. But, often, there aren't enough people to make sure polluters obey the rules, and the problems continue or get worse.

The polluted planet
The map shows levels of carbon dioxide pollution around the world. Carbon dioxide is produced when fuels such as coal and gasoline are burned to provide power for factories and transport. It is one of the greenhouse gases that cause global warming (see page 31). In many big cities, road traffic is responsible for a high percentage of carbon dioxide pollution.

The air we breathe
Vehicles, power stations and factories belch out gases and other substances such as soot and oil droplets. These combine and react in sunlight to produce a smoky fog called smog. It clouds the view, chokes people and animals and increases breathing and lung conditions such as asthma, bronchitis, pneumonia and cancers.

NORTH AMERICA

87%

Los Angeles

80%

Mexico City

SOUTH AMERICA

86%

São Paulo

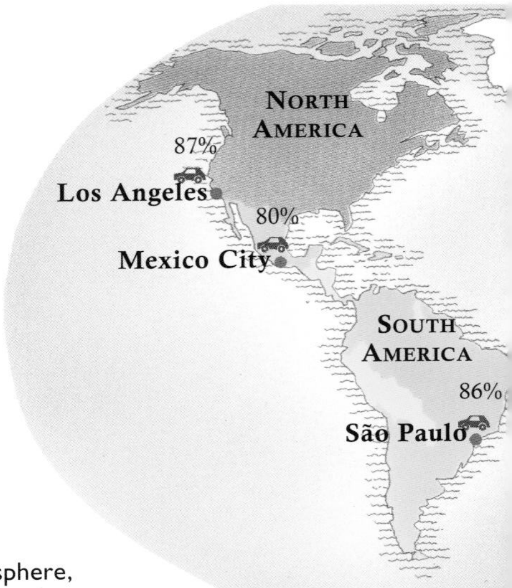

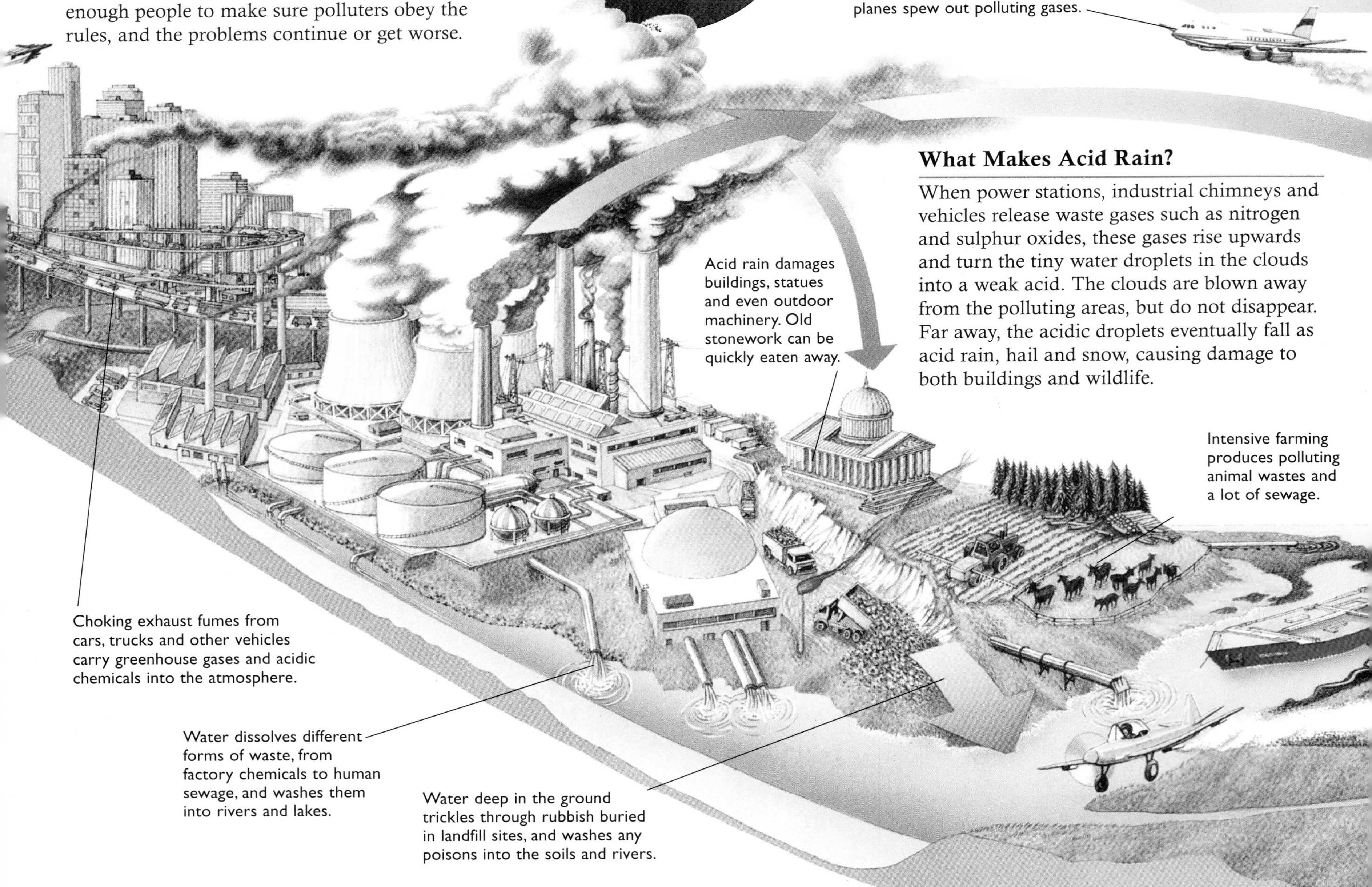

Even high up in the atmosphere, planes spew out polluting gases.

What Makes Acid Rain?

When power stations, industrial chimneys and vehicles release waste gases such as nitrogen and sulphur oxides, these gases rise upwards and turn the tiny water droplets in the clouds into a weak acid. The clouds are blown away from the polluting areas, but do not disappear. Far away, the acidic droplets eventually fall as acid rain, hail and snow, causing damage to both buildings and wildlife.

Acid rain damages buildings, statues and even outdoor machinery. Old stonework can be quickly eaten away.

Intensive farming produces polluting animal wastes and a lot of sewage.

Choking exhaust fumes from cars, trucks and other vehicles carry greenhouse gases and acidic chemicals into the atmosphere.

Water dissolves different forms of waste, from factory chemicals to human sewage, and washes them into rivers and lakes.

Water deep in the ground trickles through rubbish buried in landfill sites, and washes any poisons into the soils and rivers.

Holes in the Atmosphere

Sunshine contains many kinds of rays, including light, heat and ultra-violet (UV). Too much UV can damage people and animals, causing sunburn, skin cancers and eye cataracts. A natural form of oxygen, called ozone, forms a layer about 9-30mi up in the atmosphere. It absorbs much UV and sends its energy back into space. But industrial chemicals called CFCs, and carbon dioxide from burning fuels, destroy ozone, which means that more UV can now reach the Earth's surface (see right). Because of this, CFCs are banned in many places.

Some UV radiation passes through normal ozone layer to the Earth's surface.

Some UV radiation absorbed by ozone layer and its energy reflected back into space.

Much more radiation passes through thinned ozone layer.

ANTARCTICA

SOUTH AMERICA

Ozone "hole" is a seasonal thinning of ozone layer. Weather patterns keep it mainly above the Antarctic and Arctic, but it is slowly spreading.

CFCs move upwards and thin down ozone layer.

86%
London
EUROPE
ASIA
Athens
59%
Osaka 59%
Manila 71%
AFRICA
Kuala Lumpa 79%
INDONESIA
AUSTRALIA

The Sun – source of UV and other rays

KEY

■ High pollution	■ Low pollution		
■ Medium pollution	□ Very low pollution		
🚗 87%	Percentage of pollution caused by road traffic		

BELOW: Trees that suffer acid rain lose their leaves. Unable to absorb the Sun's energy, they soon weaken and die.

WHAT CAN WE DO TO HELP?

- Think before throwing things away – use recycling banks instead.

- Buy products with minimal packaging made from recycled or renewable materials.

- Share car journeys, and use public transport or cycle when possible.

- Don't waste energy – turn lights off when they're not needed and use low energy light bulbs.

- Cut down on heat loss with better insulation in the home.

- Take part in campaigns to help protect the environment.

Acid Rain Disaster

Acid rain has a direct and drastic effect on trees and other plants. Healthy leaves and beautiful flowers are quickly killed by the poisonous rainfall. The acids also change the chemical balance in the soil, freeing particles of aluminium that are normally combined with other substances. These wash into streams and lakes, harming fish and threatening other water creatures.

Oil tankers spill slicks of crude oil into the sea, smothering coasts and killing sea life.

Winds blow acid rain up to 1,850mi away from the polluting area, to places that were once clean and fresh.

Surges of water from melting snow carry an "acid wave" along mountain streams and rivers.

Farmland soil gets a harmful cocktail of polluted rain, pesticides and fertilizers.

SEE ALSO
Wildlife in Danger p62
Great Disasters p90

2
WILDLIFE
OF THE
WORLD

Imagine a journey from the Equator to the North Pole. You would see some of the world's greatest wildlife habitats. First the steamy rainforests, then grasslands with their herds of grazing animals, hot deserts, rivers and oceans, mountains, towering conifer forests and finally the great icy plains of the Arctic. Each habitat has its own identity with animals and plants that are specially adapted to the climate and environment. Since life first appeared on Earth, more than 3,500 million years ago, countless species have evolved, flourished and become extinct.

Zebras drinking at a waterhole in Namibia, Africa.

THE ENDS OF THE EARTH

It's difficult to imagine that life can survive at the poles, where the winters are long and dark, and temperatures can fall to below -76°F. Even during the brief summers, when daylight hours are long, temperatures barely rise above freezing point. Yet some plants and animals do survive in these harsh conditions, adapted in various ways to cope with the fierce winds, extreme cold and lack of food.

Puffin
Puffins live on turf covered sea cliffs where they build their nests in burrows. The bright colors of their bills only develop during the breeding season.

Ptarmigan in winter coat

Ptarmigan in summer coat

Sperm whale
Sperm whales dive to great depths to find their favourite food – squid. One sperm whale was found with the remains of 18,000 squid in its stomach.

ABOVE: In its white winter coat, the Arctic fox blends in with its surroundings, making it difficult for its prey to spot it as it slowly moves in for the kill.

Arctic fox in summer coat

ABOVE: As the winter snows melt, the ptarmigan and the Arctic fox change into their summer colours.

Changing Color

The Arctic landscape is almost pure white in winter but in summer it changes to greens and browns. An animal with a white coat would no longer be camouflaged in the summer. So some animals have adapted to these seasonal changes by changing color. The Arctic fox, for example, has a dense white fur in winter but, as summer comes, it slowly changes to a grey-brown. Ptarmigans, which live among the rocks of the high slopes, turn from pure white to a mottled black, red and white.

Biggest is best
Walruses live in large herds along the Arctic coast where they forage on the sea bed for clams, shrimps and other shellfish. Their tusks may grow up to 3.25ft long, and are put to good use as ice-picks and weapons, or as grappling hooks to haul the animals out of the water. Within a herd, the bull with the largest tusks becomes dominant, and all the other walruses give way to him. But if two bulls have equal-sized tusks they will fight, stabbing each other until one is defeated.

RIGHT: After feeding, walruses pull themselves on to the ice to rest. If there isn't enough room, they simply lie on top of each other!

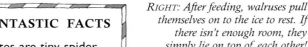

The Icy Continent

The Antarctic is a huge continent, permanently covered in ice and cut off from the rest of the world by thousands of kilometres of sea. In winter it is the most unfriendly place on Earth – dark, windy and extremely cold. So cold, in fact, that a cup of hot water freezes before you can drink it. Even in summer the temperature can drop as low as -40°F. No land mammals are found here, but many thousands of birds and seals live along the coastline. The icy waters are rich in plankton and krill (shrimp-like animals), providing a rich supply of food for penguins, seals and whales. To survive the cold, these animals insulate themselves with layers of fat, called blubber, plus thick layers of fur or feathers. The only plants are tiny red algae living in the ice, colorful lichens, and small clumps of grass growing in ice-free spots.

King penguin
Found on the islands near Antarctica, king penguins gather together in huge groups of many thousands of birds to breed and raise their young.

THE ANTARCTIC

Wandering albatross
With a wingspan of 11.5ft the wandering albatross is the world's largest seabird. It glides on air currents, hardly ever beating its wings.

Snow goose
After breeding in the Arctic summer, the snow goose flies south to the Gulf of Mexico where it spends the winter.

Walrus
A walrus's upper canine teeth are enlarged to form long white tusks. Its thick wrinkly skin helps to protect the animal against injury when it is attacked by another walrus.

THE ARCTIC

Ringed seal
One of the smallest seals, the ringed seal feeds on molluscs and fish. When it is not hunting, it pulls itself on to the ice to rest.

Ermine
The ermine, or stoat, feeds on rabbits and voles. Its winter coat is white, but in summer it turns brown with a white bib.

The Frozen North

The Arctic is a huge frozen ocean that stretches across areas of land in the far north during the winter. It is not quite as cold as the Antarctic so there is a richer variety of wildlife. The seas are teaming with fish and provide food for seals and whales, while the ice sheet itself is the haunt of large mammals such as the polar bear. During the brief summer the land becomes covered in flowers and insects which attract herds of caribou (reindeer), flocks of waterfowl and other summer visitors. But as temperatures begin to fall in the autumn, the visitors migrate south again. Only the hardiest animals, such as the musk ox and the polar bear, remain for the winter.

RIGHT: As the ground thaws, the tundra bursts into bloom.

BELOW: The map shows the polar and tundra regions of the world.

Musk ox

Golden plover

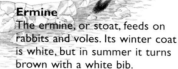

Arctic

Tundra

Tundra

Lemming

Antarctic

LEFT: Some of the plants and animals that live in the tundra regions of northern Europe.

Mountain avens

Saxifrage

Arctic poppy

Life on the Tundra

In the far north lie the tundra regions – vast treeless plains where the surface is often marshy or snow-covered, and the soil beneath frozen solid. Here, cold drying winds force the plants to grow close to the ground, usually in the shelter of rocks or small hollows where the air is still and slightly warmer. The brief summer is marked by a burst of activity when the earth thaws, plants come into flower and animals start to breed.

Leopard seal
This expert hunter swims through the chilly Antarctic waters in search of penguins to eat.

Emperor penguin
Male emperor penguins spend the dark winter on the ice shelf, each incubating a single egg. They huddle together for warmth, waiting for the females to arrive in the spring and take over.

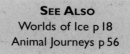

ABOVE: Leopard seals hurl an Adelie penguin into the air just for fun.

Antarctic skua
Nick-named the "pirates of the air," skuas chase other birds to steal their food. They have large, vicious-looking beaks which they use to eat other bird's eggs and chicks.

SEE ALSO
Worlds of Ice p18
Animal Journeys p56

Cold killers
There are few predators in the Antarctic, but none is more feared than the leopard seal. These vicious seals patrol the waters around the beaches where the Adelie penguins breed, waiting for chicks to take their first swim. Once they have grabbed a chick, they may play with it for up to 10 minutes before killing it. Then they smash the chick repeatedly against the surface of the water to remove its feathers before eating it.

FORESTS AND WOODLANDS

ABOVE: *In Sweden, to preserve forests, tree seedlings are planted to replace every tree cut down.*

Great coniferous, or boreal, forests stretch across the cold northern regions of North America, Europe and Asia. Further south, where the weather is milder, there are broad-leaved deciduous woodlands which undergo amazing color changes in autumn as the trees prepare to shed their leaves. Further south still, broad-leaved evergreens such as eucalyptus are found.

The Cold Coniferous Forests

Northern coniferous forests contain tall evergreen trees such as pine, spruce and fir. The branches of the trees block out most of the light so the forests are dark, and a thick layer of needles covers the forest floor, preventing smaller plants from growing. Because there is not much food, the forests are home to relatively few animals. The Canadian forest shown below shelters moose, bears, wolves and squirrels. In spring and summer a burst of insect life attracts birds which feed greedily.

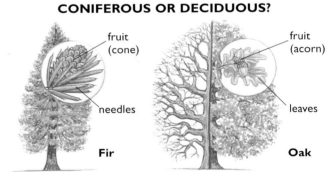

Western red cedar
Found in the forests of western USA, this conifer was once used by native Americans to make totem poles and canoes.

NORTH AMERICA

EUROPE

SOUTH AMERICA

Key

Coniferous forests

Deciduous forests

Broad-leaved evergreen forests

CONIFEROUS OR DECIDUOUS?

fruit (cone)

needles

Fir

fruit (acorn)

leaves

Oak

Conifers are evergreens, with needle-shaped leaves that are shed throughout the year, so the tree is never bare. Deciduous trees have broader leaves that are shed in autumn. Because needles cope well with cold and snow, conifers are found in the colder parts of the world.

Yellow-bellied sapsucker

Great horned owl

Moose

Grey wolves

Wolverine

Black bear

Red squirrel

Two-barred Crossbill

Wood ant

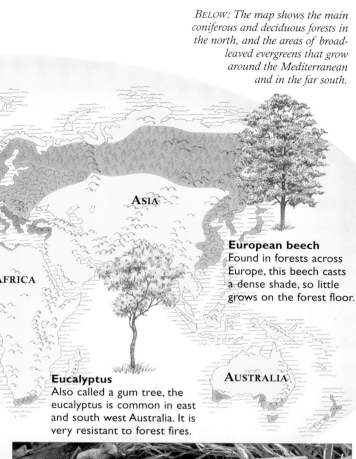

BELOW: The map shows the main coniferous and deciduous forests in the north, and the areas of broad-leaved evergreens that grow around the Mediterranean and in the far south.

European beech
Found in forests across Europe, this beech casts a dense shade, so little grows on the forest floor.

Eucalyptus
Also called a gum tree, the eucalyptus is common in east and south west Australia. It is very resistant to forest fires.

FANTASTIC FACTS

• The world's biggest tree is the "General Sherman," a giant sequoia in Sequoia National Park, California. It stands 275ft tall, and has a girth of 103ft. Its timber would make 5,000 million matches!

• The world's tallest tree was a eucalyptus which is believed to have reached a height of 459ft in 1885.

SEE ALSO
Tropical Rainforests p 42
Life Among the Peaks p 44

Beaver enters lodge via underwater entrance

Dam

Lodge

Chamber

Raised water level

Central island built of logs, twigs, stones and mud

Building a New Home

Beavers once lived throughout the northern coniferous forests, but now they are only found in North America. Before it can build its home, the beaver has to create a new lake by damming a stream. The dam is made from felled logs and twigs, covered by stones and gravel, and finished with a waterproof layer of mud. Once the lake has formed, the beaver builds its home, or lodge, in the middle of it. The lodge may look like a heap of sticks, but it has underwater entrances leading to a chamber that lies just above water level. The beaver's lodge is warm in winter and safe from predators.

Deciduous Woodlands

Broad-leaved deciduous woods have a mix of deciduous trees, such as oak, beech and maple. The trees form a leafy roof, or canopy, below which smaller shrubs grow, and the ground is covered by leaf litter (fallen leaves) and low-growing plants, many of which burst into flower in the spring. The scene below shows a typical European woodland during the summer, rich in wildlife such as foxes, badgers, deer and birds. But in winter, the trees will be bare and the woods will appear lifeless.

A Winter's Sleep

Long cold winters create problems for many small animals. They can't find enough food to eat or keep their bodies warm. So, in order to survive, some go into a deep sleep called hibernation. Before hibernating, the dormouse (above) eats lot of nuts and becomes very fat. Then it finds a dry, safe place to curl up and sleep. Its body temperature falls and its heart beat slows until it wakes in the spring, when the weather is warmer.

ABOVE: Koalas are only found in Australia. They are adapted to life in trees and live on a diet of leaves, especially eucalyptus leaves.

Greater spotted woodpecker

Sparrowhawk

Red fox

Roe deer

Wild boar

Brown hairstreak

Silver wash fritillary

Wood mouse

Badger

Stag beetle

TROPICAL RAINFORESTS

Rainforests are hot and steamy places. The atmosphere is thick with moisture and waters drips from every surface. The sound of animals calling to each other fills the air, but you can't see a living creature in the gloom. Nowhere else on Earth can you find such a rich variety of wildlife as you can in the tropical rainforests – these forests cover only 6% of the Earth's surface, but they are home to more than half of the world's plant and animal species.

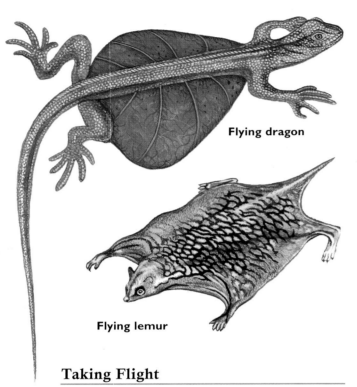

Flying dragon

Flying lemur

ABOVE: Heavy rainfall often makes the forest floor swampy, and streams are common. This stream in an Australian rainforest has created a small gap in the canopy, allowing the sunlight through.

RIGHT: A tiny number of the many thousands of species that live in the Amazon rainforests. Forests can be divided into three different layers – the canopy, shrub and ground layer – each one home to a different range of plants and animals.

Taking Flight

Some forest animals, such as the flying squirrels and tree frogs of South America, and the flying lemurs and dragons of South East Asia (above), can actually glide from tree to tree. The flying dragon feeds on ants in the canopy, but it does not like climbing downwards! Instead, it launches itself into the air, extending the flaps of skin between its legs so that they act like wings. Having landed on a tree lower down, the dragon then climbs up, eating ants as it goes. When it reaches the top it starts all over again.

Riches of the Amazon

The Amazon rainforests are incredibly rich in wildlife. In an area the size of a football field (1.5 acres), you may find more than 100 different species of tree and several hundred types of insect. There are monkeys, birds and bats in the canopy, feeding on leaves and fruit. And on the ground, big cats such as the jaguar hunt for prey.

Ferocious fish

Despite being only 2-8 inches long, piranha are among the world's most vicious fish. They live in the rivers of South America where they hunt in shoals, sending out a scout to select a victim before the rest of the shoal moves in, attracted by the smell of blood. The piranha rip their prey to pieces, pulling off small bits of flesh with their extremely sharp teeth. They have been known to strip a cow to its bones in just five minutes!

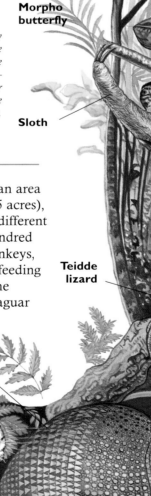

Hummingbird

Toucan

Morpho butterfly

Sloth

Teidde lizard

Giant armadillo

Jaguar

Harpy eagle

Palm

Rainforests of the world

Tropical forests are found in the hot, wet equatorial zones between the tropics of Cancer and Capricorn. There is usually a heavy rainfall here, and temperatures are high all year round, with little difference between seasons. Two-thirds of the total rainforest area is in the Amazon Basin, while the rest lies in central Africa, South East Asia, New Guinea and Australia. Unfortunately, as this map shows, vast areas of rainforest have already been destroyed, and by the year 2000 more than half of the world's rainforests may have been lost.

Tropic of Cancer

Equator

Tropic of Capricorn

Key ▨ Areas originally covered by rainforest ▨ Existing areas of rainforest

Liana

Life in the canopy
The rainforest canopy rises to a height of 130ft, with just a few trees, called emergents, rising above the rest. Animals use the network of interlocking branches as highways to move through the forest. Because it is so rich in food, the canopy is home to most of the forest's life, including birds, mammals, snakes, frogs and insects.

Scarlet macaw

Spider monkey

HIDE AND SEEK

Orchid mantis

With so many predators in the forest, some animals use camouflage to help them blend in with their surroundings so they won't be seen. The chameleon is a master of camouflage. Its skin contains lots of different pigments so it can quickly change its color to match that of its background. The orchid mantis uses another type of camouflage, known as mimicry. It looks just like an orchid, so would-be predators don't give it a second glance.

Chameleon

The shrub layer
The canopy blocks out most of the light so only a few plants such as palms can survive lower down. Where there is a gap, and hence more light, shrubs and lianas (climbing plants) grow. Snakes, lizards, spiders and leeches live here, waiting to drop on the animals below.

Bird-eating spider

Emerald tree boa

Poison arrow frog

The ground layer
The ground is gloomy and damp, and only plants such as mosses and ferns can grow. The forest floor is covered with fallen leaves, fruits and nuts which fall down from above. Beetles, ants and fungi live here, breaking down the dead and decaying matter, and recycling it.

Ichneumon butterfly

ABOVE: The attractive ring-tailed lemur lives in the rainforest canopy where it feeds on leaves and fruit. Found only in Madagascar, lemurs are small primates (related to apes and monkeys), with long bushy tails.

ABOVE: Natives of South America hunt using deadly darts tipped with poison from the poison arrow frog.

SEE ALSO
Climate and Weather p 30
Wildlife in Danger p 62

FANTASTIC FACTS

• The brightly colored poison arrow frog of South America has glands that make one of the world's deadliest animal poisons. It is so lethal that less than 0.00001g can kill a human.

• The Malaysian monster flower, or rafflesia, is the world's largest flower, up to 3.25ft across. You wouldn't want to stand too close to it though – it stinks of rotting flesh!

Rafflesia

LIFE AMONG THE PEAKS

Mountains form the most spectacular scenery on Earth. If you climb up from the valleys into the peaks, the temperature drops, the air thins, and the sunlight becomes stronger. Mountain weather is changeable, and life is harsh for animals and plants. They have to survive strong winds and long, cold winters, when food is in short supply, or buried beneath the snow. The summers are warmer but very short.

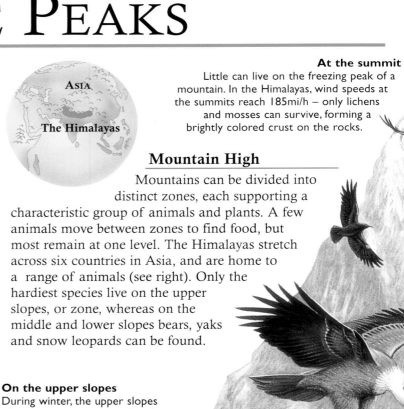

At the summit
Little can live on the freezing peak of a mountain. In the Himalayas, wind speeds at the summits reach 185mi/h – only lichens and mosses can survive, forming a brightly colored crust on the rocks.

Mountain High

Mountains can be divided into distinct zones, each supporting a characteristic group of animals and plants. A few animals move between zones to find food, but most remain at one level. The Himalayas stretch across six countries in Asia, and are home to a range of animals (see right). Only the hardiest species live on the upper slopes, or zone, whereas on the middle and lower slopes bears, yaks and snow leopards can be found.

LEFT: The mountain gorilla is a rare species, in danger of extinction.

BELOW: The hyrax is the elephant's closest relative!

On the upper slopes
During winter, the upper slopes of a mountain are covered with a blanket of snow called a "snowfield." Alpine plants grow slowly here, nestling between the rocks. Insects are blown to the upper slopes where they fall prey to spiders.

The Mountains of Africa

The highest mountain in Africa is Mount Kilimanjaro, which rises from the tropical grasslands of Tanzania in the East of the continent to a towering height of 19,340ft. The mountain gorilla and the hyrax can be found in the tropical forest that clothes the lower slopes of some African mountains while, higher up, the steep slopes are covered in weird alpine plants. These are often giants compared with their lowland relatives.

On the middle slopes
Colorful meadows are found on the steep slopes below the snowfields. Summer is short, so the plants flower and set seed in just four months. In early summer, these meadows seem full of flowers and abound with insects.

Tibetan yak

Red panda

Blue magpie

Life on the lower slopes
The lower slopes are covered by forest. The trees only grow up to 11,155ft – the treeline – beyond which it is too cold and the soil is too thin. In the Himalayas, the uppermost forests are coniferous, with cedar, pine and fir trees, while deciduous forests of oak and rhododendron are found in the sheltered valleys.

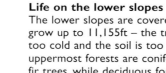

The Panda at Risk

The giant panda is one of the world's rarest mammals, with fewer than 1,000 left in the mountains of central and southern China. Recently, their numbers have fallen because growth of the bamboo on which they feed has slowed down, something that happens every 100 years. Much of the panda's habitat has also been destroyed.

Giant panda

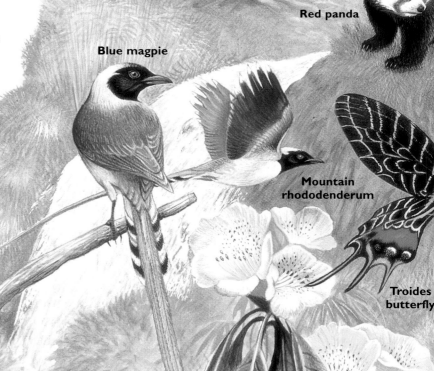

Bearded vulture

Mountain rhododenderum

Troides butterfly

Life in the Alps

The Alps stretch across central Europe and create a landscape of ice-capped peaks and forested slopes. The word "alp" means mountain pasture, where cattle graze in summer. On the higher slopes, it is possible to spot the chamois. This nimble animal leaps down the steepest of rock faces to escape predators such as the bear or wolf. A newly born kid can follow its mother along narrow rock ledges and across rocky slopes within hours of birth.

EUROPE
Habitat of chamois

Chamois

SEE ALSO
Mountain Building p 16
Worlds of Ice p 18

Himalayan Griffon

MOUNTAIN SURVIVORS

Alpine plants have to survive cold, snow, drought, strong sunlight and wind! So only specialized plants are found on mountain peaks. Their leaves of are either arranged in a rosette or form a cushion, and they are often covered in white hairs that protect them against frost. Many plants are low-growing, finding shelter in crevices and between rocks. One exception is the giant lobelia of Africa which grows over 3ft tall.

Lady's mantle

Edelweiss

Giant lobelia

American Hard Rock

The Rockies are a famous mountain range that form a craggy barrier dividing the continent of North America in two. They stretch from New Mexico, in the south, to the Yukon in Canada, in the north. Among the spectacular high peaks are glaciers and vast fields of ice. The Rockies are home to a large variety of mammals including grizzly bears, mountain lions (also called pumas), bighorn sheep, and mountain goats.

NORTH AMERICA
Habitat of mountain lion

BELOW: The mountain goat has thick white fur which keeps it warm and provides camouflage against the snow. If pursued by a predator such as the mountain lion, it hides on steep cliffs where the lion cannot follow.

Mountain lion

Mountain goats

Snow leopard

Markhor

Snow partridge

Brown bear

FANTASTIC FACTS

• Insects called springtails can survive being frozen in a glacier for up to three years.

• A large mountain bird called the lammergeier feeds on bone marrow, which it gets by dropping bones from a great height on to rocks to break them open.

• Snow covered mountains may look red from a distance. This is because tiny single-celled algae in the snow contain a red pigment that protects them against the strong sunlight.

Mighty Mountain Chain

The Andes form a chain of mountains that extend down the length of South America – a massive distance of 4,040mi. Many unusual animals live among these mountains, including several types of wild camel, such as the llama and vicuna. These animals have coats of fine wool that give excellent insulation against the severe winter weather.

BELOW: Few birds can fly among the windy Andean peaks, but with its 10ft wingspan, the condor is powerful enough to soar for hours.

SOUTH AMERICA
Habitat of condor

ON THE GRASSY PLAINS

Grasslands are vast open plains where trees and bushes are rare. They are home to huge herds of grazing mammals, and beneath the surface the soil is honeycombed with the tunnels of burrowing animals. The world's grasslands lie either side of the deserts, and cover more than one quarter of the Earth's land surface. Tropical grasslands are hot all year round but temperate grasslands, which lie nearer the poles, have hot and cold seasons.

Insects for Supper

Grasslands are teeming with insects, and many animals exist solely on an insect diet. The giant anteater, which lives in the South American llanos, eats large ground-dwelling carpenter ants. The anteater finds them by their smell, and uses its powerful claws to rip open the nest before licking up the ants with its tongue. It's careful not to take too many though, so it can return another day.

South American anteater

Key
Tropical grasslands
Temperate grasslands

Bison
Bison roam the grasslands in herds of 10-20 animals, looking for fresh grazing.

Coyote
Looking like a small wolf, the coyote is a predator of the prairies.

PRAIRIES

Rattle snake
This poisonous snake warns its enemies to stay away by rattling the dead scales on the end of its tail.

Hyena
Hyenas are scavengers that hunt in packs. One group was seen to eat a zebra in just 15 minutes.

Burrowing owl
The burrowing owl lives underground, emerging at night to hunt for lizards.

LLANOS

SAVANNAH

Viscacha
This large, long-tailed burrowing rodent lives in colonies on the pampas.

PAMPAS

Pampas deer
One of the largest grazing mammals on the pampas, this deer is now endangered.

African Elephant
Elephants may eat up to 330lbs of food and drink 26 gallons of water in a day.

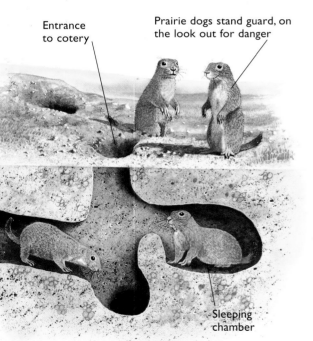

Entrance to cotery

Prairie dogs stand guard, on the look out for danger

Sleeping chamber

Town Life

There is nowhere to hide on the North American prairies and small animals are easily spotted by predators such as eagles or coyotes. They can't outrun their enemies, so many animals seek shelter underground. Prairie dogs dig burrows where they live and rear their young in safety. These hamster-like rodents live together in highly organized groups called coteries, several of which make up a town. The towns may cover 160 acres (130 soccer fields!), and contain hundreds of interconnecting burrows. When prairie dogs go above ground to feed, one or two stand on guard duty, looking out for predators.

ATHLETES OF THE BIRD WORLD

Grasslands are home to the world's largest birds – flightless birds such as the African ostrich, the South American rhea and the Australian emu. Their powerful long legs enable the birds to see above the tall grass and to run fast. The ostrich is both the largest bird, reaching up to 9ft and weighing 340lbs and the fastest – it can run at up to 40mi/h.

Emu

Rhea

Ostrich

Life on the Steppes

The temperate grasslands of Eastern Europe and Russia are called the steppes. Here, the summers are hot and dry but, in winter, temperatures plummet to -4°F in the cold winds. Grasses only survive by having deep roots, which can reach water, and tough stems to withstand the wind. Herds of grazing mammals, including bison, saiga and camels (above), feed on the grass. Predators, such as bears and wolves, stay hidden during the day, only emerging at night to hunt under the cover of darkness. These temperate grasslands have rich soils, so much original grassland has now been ploughed up and replaced by wheat fields.

BELOW: The map shows the main tropical and temperate grasslands of the world and some of the animals that live there.

Giraffe

Elephant

Gerenuk

Dik-dik

Hamster
Hamsters carry food in their cheek pouches and store it underground until it is needed. One store was found to contain 200lbs of food!

STEPPES

Great bustard
Found on the steppes, the great bustard if one of the largest flying birds, weighing in at 39lbs.

Saiga
A goat-like antelope of the steppes, the saiga has a thick, woolly coat to keep it warm during the cold winters.

Kangaroo
Kangaroos spend the day under the cover of trees, emerging at night to graze on grass and other plants.

AUSTRALIAN GRASSLANDS

Common eland
The largest of the antelopes, the eland has large spiral horns up to 3.25ft long. It lives in heards of up to 100 individuals.

Food for All
Herbivores do not all eat the same food – some eat different plants, others eat the same plant at different heights. This way they are not all competing with each other. In the African savannah, for example, the acacia tree may be eaten by four different animals (see left), each one eating leaves at a different level. The giraffe, with its long neck, eats the highest leaves, but the tiny dik-dik can only reach the lowest ones.

SEE ALSO
Climate and Weather p 30
Wildlife in Danger p 62

RIGHT: Australia's compass termite always builds its slab-like mound facing east/west.

FANTASTIC FACTS

• A giant anteater's tongue is 24in long and can reach out 150 times a minute to lick up ants.

• The cheetah is the fastest animal on Earth. It can reach speeds of up to 62mi/h, but only in short bursts.

• Giraffe are always on the lookout for their enemies. They only sleep for 20 minutes each night, split into three or four short naps.

Tropical dustmen
Termites are like the dustmen of tropical grasslands. They build huge mounds where millions of them live together in a colony. Each day thousands of worker termites leave the nest to hunt for dead leaves which they carry back into their nest. Because they can't digest the leaves themselves, they grow fungi to break the leaves down into other substances that they *can* eat.

The Tropical Savannah

The tropical grasslands, or savannah, of East Africa are one of the world's most spectacular habitats. In the dry season they are golden and parched dry, and herds of animals gather around the water holes. But all this changes after the rains. Grass begins to grow, the landscape becomes green, and flowers appear. The savannah supports vast numbers of grazing animals, such as antelope, zebra, wildebeest and the world's largest land mammals – elephants and rhinos. These in turn attract predators such as lions and cheetahs.

Rhinoceros

Wildebeest

Weaver birds

Springbok

Cheetah

Giraffe

Lions

Zebra

Animals gather around a water hole in the African savannah.

WETLAND WILDLIFE

Ponds, streams, estuaries and swamps are just a few of the many types of wetland that can be found throughout the world. Wetlands are places where water collects, either permanently or for only short periods of time. The water may be fresh, as in the Florida Everglades, or salty as in the French Camargue. Wetlands are rich habitats, home to countless different kinds of fish, birds and aquatic organisms. But they are continually being destroyed and are probably the most threatened places in the world.

The mighty Pantanal
The Pantanal (left) is one huge patchwork of marsh, river, lake and grassland. It spans the border of Brazil and Bolivia, covering an area half the size of France. From November to May much of the land is under water, and spectacular numbers of waterbirds gather here to feed. The area is also home to jaguars, marsh deer and caimans (related to alligators).

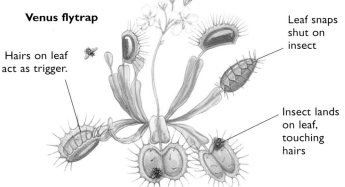

Venus flytrap

Hairs on leaf act as trigger.

Leaf snaps shut on insect

Insect lands on leaf, touching hairs

Flies for supper
Many wetland plants can't get enough food from the ground, so they get what they need by catching insects! The Venus flytrap is found in the Everglades. It has very sensitive hairs on its leaves that act like a trigger when they are touched. If an insect lands on a leaf and knocks the hairs, the leaf snaps shut, trapping the insect inside where it is digested by the plant.

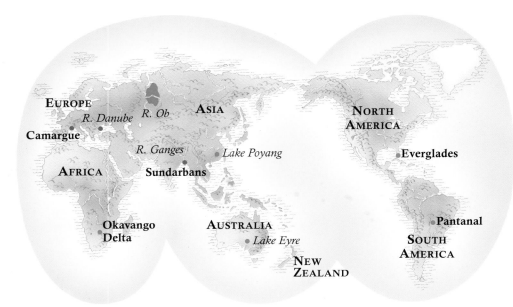

ABOVE: The map shows some of the major wetland areas of the world. Those lying along the coastline are covered in salt water but inland wetlands, such as the flood plains of rivers, contain fresh water.

KEY

- Freshwater wetlands
- Saltwater wetlands

The changing landscape
A pond or lake does not stay the same for ever. Mud gradually builds up, and the edges of the pond become shallow and muddy (1). Reeds begin to grow around the edges, their roots trapping more and more mud. Soon the reeds grow in towards the middle of the pond (2) until, eventually, the water is choked with them. By now the water has become very shallow and small shrubs and trees have started to grow on the drier areas(3). Finally, the lake disappears altogether and is replaced by a wet woodland, supporting a new range of wildlife.

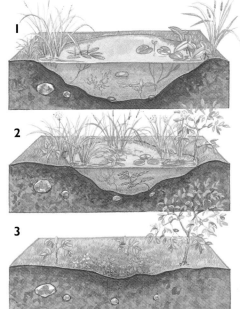

FANTASTIC FACTS

- Vast areas of mangrove swamp along the Indonesian coast are to be cleared for pulpwood, even though the fish that live there could earn up to seven times as much money in exports.

- Findland is one of the wettest countries: 11% is covered by 55,000 lakes and a further 30% is bog.

- Once thought to eat their young, crocodiles are now known to carry their young around in their mouths.

The Grassy Waters

The Everglades in Florida (above) is one of the world's largest freshwater marshes. Native Americans called it grassy waters because it was like a river of grass creeping towards the sea. The flat plains are covered by saw grass which reach 13ft high, and fish, frogs and alligators live among the pools. Today, more than half of the original Everglades has been drained to make way for farms or towns.

BELOW: Hippos spend the day in the Okavango Delta lying in the water or wallowing in mud. At night they leave the water to graze on the grass.

The Okavango Delta

The gull-like cry of the African fish eagle is one of the most beautiful sounds of the Okavango Delta. This vast area of swamp and grassland in Botswana, southern Africa, is an oasis for thousands of birds and mammals, including some of Africa's rarest species, such as the shoebill stork. Hippos are very common, as too are kingfishers, egrets and herons.

Life in the Carmargue

The Camargue is famous for its black bulls, white horses and pink flamingoes. It is a flat landscape of salt marshes, muddy creeks and salt pans (small saltwater pools). The conservation of the flamingo has been a great success, and the number of breeding birds has increased six-fold over the last 50 years. But it is a constant battle to make sure that the thousands of visitors that come each year don't do too much damage to this fragile habitat.

ABOVE: These flamingoes get the pink color of their plumage from the small aquatic animals they eat.

SEE ALSO
Lakes and Caves p 22
Life Beneath the Waves p 52

Archer fish

The water pistol fish
The archer fish of South East Asia has an unusual way of catching prey. It looks out for a spider or insect resting on an overhanging branch, then squirts a jet of water from its mouth, knocking its victim into the water where it can easily be caught.

Submerged by the Tide

Mangrove swamps, such as the Sundarbans of India, are found in tropical coastal regions. The mangrove trees from which they get their name have roots that form a floating raft on top of the mud. The tide dominates life in the swamp. Twice a day it retreats, and twice a day it rises, submerging the land. At low tide, hordes of animals emerge to feed on the food left behind by the tide. A smell of rotting matter fills the air, flies dodge everywhere, and water drips from the trees. When the tide returns, the animals seek refuge in burrows or climb the trees.

Proboscis monkey
This monkey is named after the huge, droopy nose of the male, which straightens out when the male makes his loud, honking cry!

Indian elephant
Easy to train, the Indian elephant is often used to carry people and goods around the wetlands.

Snake
Many mangrove snakes are good swimmers and can catch fish.

Tiger
In the late afternoon, the tiger starts its silent hunt for prey, seeking out deer and boar.

Crocodile
This is the world's largest reptile, growing throughout its long life. Some live up to 100 years, and grow 15ft in length.

Mudskipper
This fish looks like a large tadpole. It can leave the water and wiggle across the mud using its front fins.

Fiddler crab
These crabs emerge from their burrows at low tide. The male has one claw larger than the other which it waves it at the female to get her attention.

DESERT SURVIVAL

Deserts are vast, dry wildernesses. They may seem empty but, surprisingly, quite a few plants and animals make their home in these barren places. Deserts may be sandy or rocky, hot or cold, but all suffer from a shortage of water, and only those species well adapted to the conditions can survive. Plants and animals have developed various ways of going for long periods without water – desert plants may store water, whereas many animals live off the water contained in their food.

LEFT: The arrival of rain brings a quick change to the desert. Plants that bloom every year begin to grow and, within a few weeks, the once bare ground is covered with colorful plants. They live for just one season, during which time they must flower and produce seeds before the moisture in the soil dries up.

Arizona Hot Spots

The Arizona Desert in the USA (shown below) is hot and dry. Cloudless skies mean that the desert heats up during the day, and the temperature may reach 122°F. But at night the lack of clouds allows heat to escape into space and the temperature rapidly plummets to freezing. Cacti are very common here – certain species, such as the saguaro, grow as big as a tree. Some are so large that animals, such as the elf owl, make their homes inside them. Other animals dig burrows where they can escape from the heat and build their nests. A number of creatures, including the scorpion, gila monster and tarantula, are poisonous, so they can protect themselves from other hungry predators.

Elf owl

Saguaro cactus

Thirsty work
Desert plants have to be able to survive long periods without water. When the rains come, they absorb as much water as possible and store it, often in their barrel-shaped trunks. Many desert plants have tough spines instead of leaves to cut down on water loss, and some are covered in long, shining white hairs that help reflect the blistering heat.

Trapdoor spider
This spider hides in its burrow, beneath a trapdoor, waiting to pounce on prey.

Yucca
A large desert plant, the yucca has thick, waxy leaves and bell-shaped flowers.

Cobra
The cobra squirts deadly venom at its enemies.

ARIZONA DESERT

Bobcat
The bobcat hunts mainly at night and is a good climber.

Secretary bird
A long-legged bird that kills snakes by stamping on them.

SAHARA DESERT

Fennec fox
With its huge ears, the fennec can hear the slightest sound.

Fairy armadillo
A nocturnal burrowing mammal, covered in bony plates that protect it from its enemies.

NAMIB DESERT

ATACAMA DESERT

Welwitschia
This plant gets its water from the fog that drifts over the Namib Desert from the coast.

Hedgehog cactus

Greater roadrunner

Arizona coral snake

Desert tortoise

Coyote

Giant desert hairy scorpion with young

Chilling Out in the Gobi

The Gobi is a huge inland desert that stretches across China and Mongolia. It is cold and sometimes snowy – for six months of the year, temperatures drop below freezing. Herds of grazing animals, such as wild camels and horses, live here, their thick coats insulating them against the cold. Camels can drink up to 37 gallons of water in one go, then live for a week without drinking.

Bactrian camel

BELOW: The map shows the world's main desert regions, and some of the animals and plants that live there.

KEEPING COOL

During the fierce heat of the day, many desert animals, such as this jerboa, seek refuge in the cool shade of burrows that they dig in the sand. They remain hidden from would-be hunters until nightfall, when it is safe for them to come out and search for food.

Jerboa

Life in the Sahara

Much of the Sahara Desert that stretches across North Africa is covered in sand, and water holes are scarce. Herds of grazing mammals, such as the addax, are active early in the morning and evening, but rest in the shade during the day. An addax can last as long as a year without drinking, because it gets all the water it needs from plants and dew. Huge herds of addax once roamed across the Sahara, but today only a few herds remain. The rest have been hunted.

Addax

GOBI DESERT

Przewalskis horse
This horse once roamed the Gobi Desert in herds, but none has been seen here since 1968. There are plans to reintroduce it.

Arabian Oryx
A beautiful antelope, now almost extinct in the wild.

A quick frill
Lizards are common in Australia, particularly in the desert regions. The Australian frilled lizard has a startling way of frightening its predators. When it's threatened, it erects a brightly colored frill in a fan around its head, then it hisses angrily and lashes its long tail!

Frilled lizard

SEE ALSO
Deserts Hot and Cold p 26
Climate and Weather p 30

Dingo
A wild dog of Australia that is known to hunt kangaroos in packs.

AUSTRALIAN DESERT

Spadefoot toad

FANTASTIC FACTS

• The saguaro cactus grows up to 50ft tall, and stores several tons of water in its stem.

• A spadefoot toad can loose up to 60% of its body weight while it remains buried underground, waiting for the rains to begin.

• The world's hottest air temperature, recorded on September 13, 1922, in the Sahara Desert, was a sweltering 136°F.

Waterholding frog
Swollen with water, this frog burrows underground, waiting for the next rains.

Race against time
Just as the last of the desert pools dry up in North Africa, the spadefoot toad buries itself in the sand with its shovel-shaped feet. It stays underground without food until the rains come, when it digs itself out. Then it's a race against time – there are only a few weeks in which the toad must breed and lay its eggs, and the tadpoles must mature into young toads, before the pools dry up again.

Teddy bear cholla

Desert kangaroo rat

Gila monster

Desert tarantula

RIGHT: Desert racing is becoming a popular sport in some countries. People may not think they cause any damage by driving across the desert, but the terrain is actually very fragile. Often, the surface of the sand forms a thin crust which protects the ground below. Driving across the desert destroys this protective crust. The sand then blows away, exposing the delicate roots of plants which causes them to die.

LIFE BENEATH THE WAVES

ABOVE: Since the earliest times, stories have been told of huge sea monsters that attack ships and drag them beneath the waves. Could these monsters have been nothing but giant squids, which grow up to 60ft long?

The sea is immense, covering more than two-thirds of the Earth's surface. Apart from the uppermost layer, the water is dark and cold, yet even in this gloom a huge range of animals and plants are found. The open waters of the ocean can be divided into three distinct zones, each with its own wildlife. Many of the deepest oceans still have to be explored and scientists are discovering weird new life forms in their depths.

BELOW: Many fish swim in shoals, because a large group of fish is less likely to be attacked by a predator than a single fish. If a shoal is attacked, it may divide in two, or split up and scatter in all directions, to confuse the attacker.

The Euphotic Zone (0-325ft)

This is the uppermost level of the oceans. It is bathed in sunlight and the water is full of microscopic life called plankton. Plant plankton, or phytoplankton, is able to make its own food using the energy of the Sun. It is eaten by the zooplankton – tiny animals including the larvae of jellyfish, fish, and small shrimp-like creatures called krill. A wide range of fish and other animals, including some whales, feed off the zooplankton.

The Bathyal Zone (650-6,500ft)

Here, light levels slowly decrease to total darkness. There are fish and large mammals, but no plants. What little food there is comes from the few plankton, or wastes from above. Most animals are good hunters – they have to be or they will be hunted themselves. The fish tend to be small, with excellent senses, strong jaws and powerful teeth. They also have a huge gut, since a single meal may have to last some time.

The Abyssal Zone (6,500ft plus)

The abyssal zone is a cold and eerie place. The few creatures that are found here have adapted to life in total darkness and under enormous pressure. There is very little food, so animals have to catch whatever is available. Most fish are small, white or grey in color, and blind. But they are very sensitive to touch and taste. Some have light-emitting bacteria living in their bodies, and they use the light to lure other fish into their mouths.

FANTASTIC FACTS

• A deep sea fish called the great swallower can dislocate its jaw so it can swallow fish much larger than itself.

• Giant worms that grow over 7ft long form living forests around vents of hot gas that erupt from the sea bed.

• So little is known about life in the deep that there may be as many as 10 million new species waiting to be discovered.

Basking shark

Herring

Sperm whale

Octopus

Tuna

Cod

Scarlet prawns

① **Rat-tail** ② **Glass sponge** ③ **Angler fish** ④ **Brittlestar**

Saving the Whales

For hundreds of years the great whales, such as blue and sperm whales, were hunted for their oils and meat. So many were killed that their numbers plummeted to dangerously low levels. Many species of whale became endangered. Now, thanks to worldwide bans, whaling is largely an industry of the past, and more people want to watch whales than to hunt them.

ABOVE: Once a whale has been harpooned, it is pulled alongside the boat and dragged up on a ramp. Then it is butchered.

Life on the edge

At the edge of each continent, beneath the sea, lies a ledge of land called the continental shelf (see map). Here, the water is shallow and there is plenty of light. These areas are rich in wildlife and have become important fishing grounds.

ARCTIC OCEAN

ATLANTIC OCEAN

PACIFIC OCEAN

INDIAN OCEAN

SOUTHERN OCEAN

Continental shelf

SEE ALSO
Oceans and seas p 24
Riches of the Reefs p 54

Blue whale

Leopard seal

Compass jellyfish

Sardines

Krill

Phytoplankton

Halibut

Swordfish

Giant squid

Hatchet fish

Lantern fish

The ocean food cycle

ABOVE: Called diatoms, these microscopic, single-celled plants form part of the sea's plankton.

The ocean food cycle

When sea creatures die, their bodies sink to the ocean floor where they decompose. But their nutrients (food substances) are not wasted. Cold water currents bring them back up to the surface where they are taken up by the phytoplankton. This is eaten by zooplankton, which is in turn eaten by larger animals. Then the cycle begins again.

On the Sea Floor

The sea bed is called the benthic zone. This is the most important part of the environment, because it includes the deep, oozing layer of nutrient-rich mud that covers the ocean floor. It might not look very exciting, but the mud is teeming with life, even in the deepest trenches. Scavengers, such as sea slugs, brittlestars and crabs, feed on the decomposing bodies of plants and animals. Marine worms make burrows in the mud and predatory starfish move across its surface in search of prey.

5 Grenadier fish   **6** Gulper eel   **7** Viper fish   **8** Sea cucumber

RICHES OF THE REEFS

Coral reefs are often called the rainforests of the sea because of the wealth of life that can be found living there. There are shoals of brightly colored fish, starfish, crabs, anemones and much more, all living in and around the reef. Surprising as it may seem, these reefs are made by tiny animals, called corals. They slowly build the reef over hundreds of years, forming a habitat for other animals to share.

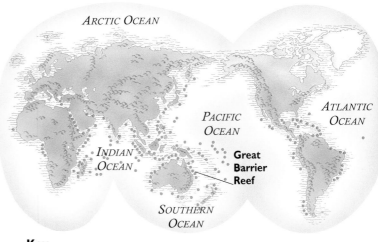

Safe and Sound

With thousands of stinging cells covering its tentacles, the sea anemone is well protected from being eaten. A touch from another animal releases a barrage of poisonous barbs that embed themselves in the attacker's body. Remarkably, the clown fish is immune to the stings, and lives happily among the sea anemone's tentacles. Its warning stripes let other fish know that, if they want to attack the clown fish, they also have to brave the tentacles of the anemone.

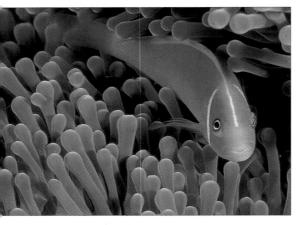

ABOVE: A clown fish seeks shelter from a sea anemone.

Key

∴ Areas of coral reef

Reefs around the world

Corals will not grow in water temperatures below 66°F, so reefs are only found in tropical and sub-tropical waters. As the map shows, they are most common in coastal areas, where there is lots of sunlight, and on a few undersea ridges. They are never found in deep water because it is too dark. Some reefs are tiny, others extend for hundreds of miles. The Great Barrier Reef, for example, stretches for 1,240mi along the east coast of Australia.

POLYPS AT WORK

Corals are colonial animals, each one made up of thousands of tiny individuals called polyps. Polyps have soft, jelly-like bodies which they protect by building a stony cup-shaped case around themselves, made of calcium carbonate (chalk). When they die their bodies decompose but the cases remain. New polyps build their cases on old ones and very slowly a reef forms, with only the outermost layer made of living coral.

Tentacles for catching food

Soft body

A coral polyp

Stony case

Tubular sponge

Brain coral

Fan coral

Olive sea snake
One of the world's most poisonous snakes.

Puffer fish
Puffs itself up to frighten away its enemies.

Sea cucumber

Sea slug

Starfish

FANTASTIC FACTS

- Coral reefs contain two-thirds of the world's species of marine fish.

- The Great Barrier Reef is so long that it can be seen from the moon.

- Corals fight for space in the reefs by using their stinging cells and poison.

- Global warming threatens to bleach and drown many reefs.

- The giant clam can weigh up to 550lbs.

How a coral atoll forms

Many reefs take the form of an atoll – a ring of coral reefs with a body of water, or lagoon, in the middle. An atoll starts life when a new volcanic island rises from the sea bed. A coral reef begins to grow in the shallow waters surrounding the island, forming what is called a fringing reef (1). If the sea level rises, the reef will grow upwards, keeping pace. Slowly, a lagoon forms between the island and the coral reef (2). If the sea continues to rise, the volcano may disappear altogether, leaving a circular reef, or atoll, enclosing a lagoon (3). Ships can only get in and out of the lagoon if there are breaks in the reef.

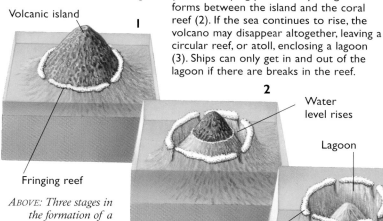

Volcanic island

1

Fringing reef

ABOVE: Three stages in the formation of a coral atoll.

2

Water level rises

Lagoon

3

Coral atoll

ABOVE: Divers enjoy exploring coral reefs because the water is warm and clear, and there is plenty to see.

Life on a Coral Reef

Corals come in all shapes, sizes and colors. There may be as many as 150 different types on just one reef. During the day, the reef is alive with thousands of fish, darting amongst the corals (see below). Many fish are poisonous, so they have warning colors. At night, predatory fish hide in crevices, so it is safer for other animals to emerge. The corals and fan worms extend their tentacles to filter out food from the water, while crabs, sea urchins and brittlestars scavenge for food.

SEE ALSO
Earthquakes & Volcanoes p 14
Wildlife in Danger p 62

Reefs at Risk

Coral reefs are popular with tourists, but tourism is putting their survival at risk. Many people travel by boat to the reefs, where the anchors can cause great damage. Divers pick up souvenirs such as coral and shells, while others may hunt sharks. In order to conserve the reefs, it is important that diving is controlled. Parts of the Great Barrier Reef are now out of bounds to divers, while elsewhere there are special anchoring points for boats.

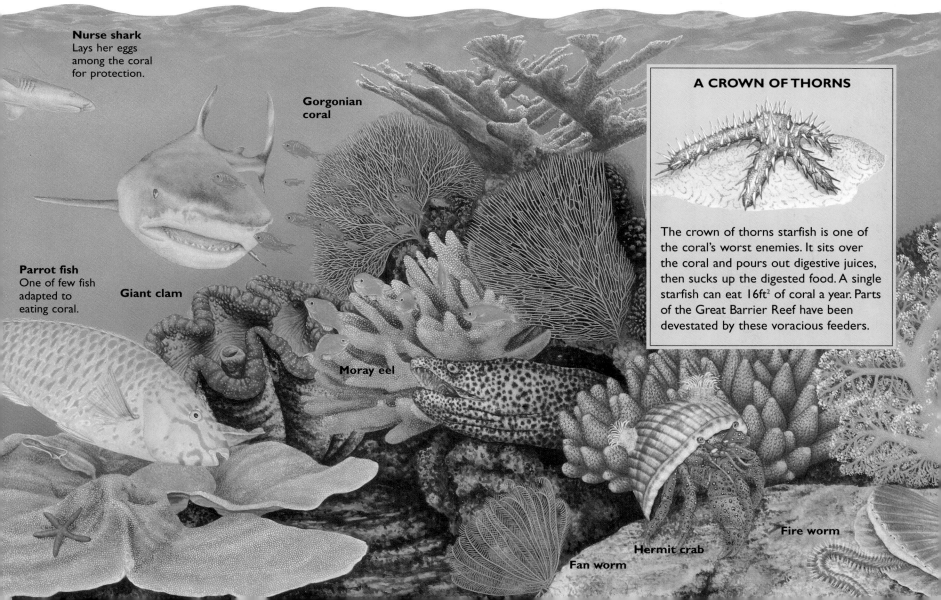

Nurse shark
Lays her eggs among the coral for protection.

Gorgonian coral

Parrot fish
One of few fish adapted to eating coral.

Giant clam

Moray eel

A CROWN OF THORNS

The crown of thorns starfish is one of the coral's worst enemies. It sits over the coral and pours out digestive juices, then sucks up the digested food. A single starfish can eat 16ft^2 of coral a year. Parts of the Great Barrier Reef have been devestated by these voracious feeders.

Fan worm

Hermit crab

Fire worm

ANIMAL JOURNEYS

Some animals undertake incredible journeys of hundreds of miles every year of their lives. They travel at the same time each year and, while some journeys may last just a few days, others may take several months. This movement is called migration, and usually involves a return journey. Some animals migrate to find food or to escape harsh winter weather, while others do so to find a mate and breed.

ABOVE: Thousands of monarch butterflies roost in the trees..

Insects on the Wing

Monarch butterflies undertake two long migrations each year. During early summer, the lengthening days act as a trigger, causing the butterflies to fly north as far as Canada, where they breed. But these butterflies don't live long enough to make the return journey, and it is their offspring that fly south in the autumn. They spend the winter in California and Mexico where, as adult butterflies, they roost in the trees in large numbers.

Family travels

Humpback whales (below) spend up to four months of the year feeding in polar waters, where there is a good supply of plankton. But these regions are too cold for new-born calves, so in autumn the whales migrate to give birth in warmer waters. They move back to the poles with their calves in spring, swimming close to the coast most of the way.

Caribou

NORTH AMERICA

SARGASSO SEA

Tundra Bound

Caribou spend the winter in the shelter of the coniferous forests of northern America. In spring, they begin their migration north to the tundra regions, where they pass the summer feeding on the rich supply of leaves and berries. But as autumn arrives, they return south again to avoid the cold polar winters.

Salmon

SOUTH AMERICA

Smelling the Way

Salmon spend their adult life at sea, but they return to the river where they were born to spawn, or breed. They have an amazing sense of smell, and can detect the characteristic smell of their home river. The salmon make their way upstream towards the source, often battling up waterfalls or over rapids to reach their destination. Once there, they mate and lay their eggs. The young fish then migrate to the sea where they mature into adults.

Marching Across the Plains

Wildebeest march many hundreds of miles in search of fresh grazing and a supply of water. Once the rains have stopped on the plains of the Serengeti, in East Africa, herds of thousands of wildebeest set off northwest to their summer feeding grounds. Many die as they attempt to cross the fast-flowing Mara river.

Wildebeest

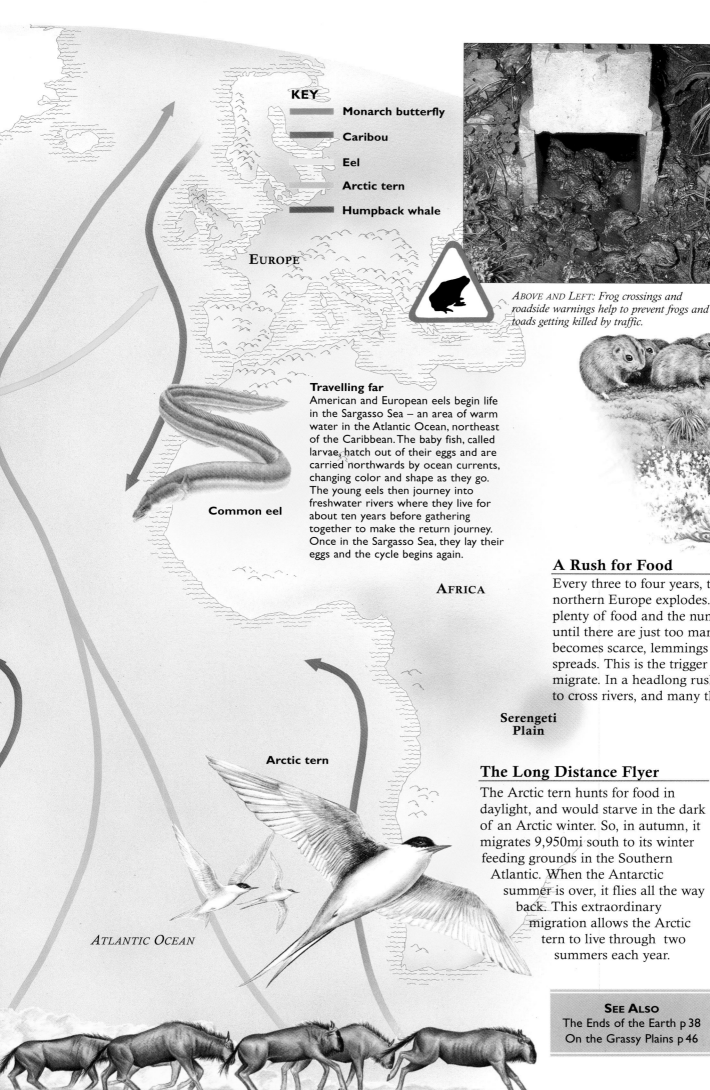

KEY

- Monarch butterfly
- Caribou
- Eel
- Arctic tern
- Humpback whale

EUROPE

AFRICA

Frog warning!
Not all migrations are long. Amphibians such as frogs and toads may only travel a few hundred feet, but the journey is essential to their survival. Frogs and toads spend the winter in hibernation, but in spring they return to water to lay their eggs, usually to a particular breeding pond. If their route takes them across a new road, many may be killed. To prevent this, road signs are be put up to warn drivers of amphibians crossing, and on busy roads, special tunnels may be built so that the animals can safely complete their journey.

ABOVE AND LEFT: Frog crossings and roadside warnings help to prevent frogs and toads getting killed by traffic.

Migrating lemmings

Travelling far
American and European eels begin life in the Sargasso Sea – an area of warm water in the Atlantic Ocean, northeast of the Caribbean. The baby fish, called larvae, hatch out of their eggs and are carried northwards by ocean currents, changing color and shape as they go. The young eels then journey into freshwater rivers where they live for about ten years before gathering together to make the return journey. Once in the Sargasso Sea, they lay their eggs and the cycle begins again.

Common eel

A Rush for Food

Every three to four years, the lemming population of northern Europe explodes. This happens when there is plenty of food and the number of lemmings increases until there are just too many animals. The result is food becomes scarce, lemmings begin to starve, and disease spreads. This is the trigger for some of the animals to migrate. In a headlong rush to find fresh food, they try to cross rivers, and many thousands die.

Serengeti Plain

Arctic tern

The Long Distance Flyer

The Arctic tern hunts for food in daylight, and would starve in the dark of an Arctic winter. So, in autumn, it migrates 9,950mi south to its winter feeding grounds in the Southern Atlantic. When the Antarctic summer is over, it flies all the way back. This extraordinary migration allows the Arctic tern to live through two summers each year.

ATLANTIC OCEAN

FANTASTIC FACTS

- Locusts travel in swarms of up to 50 million individuals, eating enough to feed 400,000 people for a year.

- Columns of migrating lemmings have been known to march through towns without stopping.

- Monarch butterflies fly a staggering 1,900mi to breed in the Canada.

- Migrating swallows can remain on the wing for over five days without stopping for rest.

SEE ALSO
The Ends of the Earth p 38
On the Grassy Plains p 46

LIFE IN THE PAST

The Earth is about 4,600 million years old but the first life forms – simple, single-celled organisms – did not appear until about 3,500 million years ago. Try to imagine all of Earth's history condensed into one year. The first primitive life would have appeared at the end of March, dinosaurs would have lived in mid-December, and humans would only have arrived a few hours before midnight on the last day of the year.

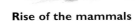

Rise of the mammals
The first mammals appeared on Earth over 220 million years ago, during the age of the dinosaurs. They were small, shy, rat-like creatures that came out at night when the dinosaurs were inactive.

Pre-Cambrian period
600 million years ago.

Sea pen

Algae

Cambrian period
570-500 million years ago. The seas were filled with many different invertebrates.

Silurian period
430-395 million years ago. The first simple plants colonized the land close to the water's edge. In the water, fish became more varied.

Trilobite

Ordovician period
500-430 million years ago. Molluscs, crustaceans and early vertebrates lived in the sea, which covered most of the Earth.

Molluscs

Jawless fish

Primitive plants

Jawed fish

Carboniferous period
345-280 million years ago. Vast forests covered low-lying swamps. They contained ferns, giant horsetails, and the first conifers. These plants eventually died and formed the coal deposits that we mine today. Amphibians were common, and the first reptiles appeared.

Giant horsetail

Conifer

Finbacked reptile   Mayfly

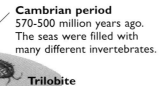

History of the Earth

Just as the day is divided into hours and minutes, the Earth's history is split into units of geological time. The divisions are eons (the longest), eras, periods, epochs, ages and chrons (the shortest). This illustration on the right shows the periods of time from the Pre-Cambrian period, which ended 570 million years ago, to the recent past. The age of rocks can be worked out by studying the type of fossils found in them.

Devonian period
395-345 million years ago. Many kinds of fish swam in the seas. On land, the first insects and amphibians appeared.

Dragonfly

Giant amphibians

Trapped in Time

When the bark of a conifer is damaged, it produces a sticky liquid called resin which eventually hardens to form amber. Millions of years ago, ancient insects walked in the resin and became trapped. As the resin hardened, the insects became encased in amber for all time. Today, scientists examining these perfectly preserved insects can discover a great deal about them.

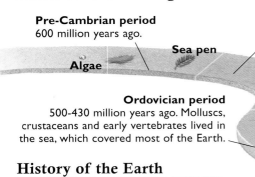

Permian period
280-245 million years ago Reptiles became more common, and the amphibians began to decline. As the Earth became drier, conifer forests replaced the swamps.

Early mammal

Early dinosaur

LEFT: A fly caught in amber offers a unique insight into prehistoric life.

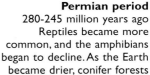

HOW FOSSILS FORM

Fossils take many millions of years to form. When a sea animal such as an ammonite died, it sank to the sea bed where it became buried in the sand (1). Soft parts of the body decayed quickly, leaving the shell behind. Layers of sand and silt built up, pressing down on the shell and the sand below (2). Eventually, the sand encasing the shell turned into rock. Over many years, the surrounding rock was worn away by erosion, revealing the fossilised shell inside (3).

Triassic period
245-208 million years ago. The climate was warm and the land formed a single huge continent. Ferns, cycads and horsetails surrounded pools, while inland conifer forests grew in desert-like conditions. The first dinosaurs appeared – they were small, lightly-built and well adapted for running. Mammals, too, came on the scene.

Mystery of the Missing Link

Nobody is quite sure if Archaeopteryx (above) is the link between birds and reptiles, or just a feathered dinosaur. We know it lived 154 million years ago during the Jurassic period, and was the size of a chicken, with both reptile and bird-like features. It had the teeth and clawed fingers of a reptile, but its wings and tail were covered in feathers like a bird.

FANTASTIC FACTS

Gigantic dragonflies lived during the Triassic period, with huge wingspans of up to 3ft.

One weird fossil animal had seven pairs of legs and seven tentacles, each tentacle ending in a mouth!

Ice ages can last up to 100,000 years. There have been 20 or so in the last 2.5 million years and another one is due soon.

A Living Fossil

In 1938, a trawler off the coast of South Africa hauled up a strange fish called a coelacanth. Until then, scientists had thought the coelacanth was extinct, so it was like finding a living dinosaur. The coelacanth is a special fish because it is related to the lungfish – the animal from which amphibians evolved. It has barely changed since the Devonian period, 345 million years ago.

ABOVE: Since the first discovery, more than 130 coelacanths have been caught and examined – some have even been filmed in the wild.

Ancient dragonfly

Modern dragonfly

THE ARCTIC

Extent of ice two million years ago

Living in an ice age

Every now and then in the Earth's history, the climate cools and the world is plunged into an ice age. When this happens, up to 40% of the land becomes covered in ice. The map shows the extent of the ice during an ice age two million years ago. The last ice age ended only 10,000 years ago.

SEE ALSO
Continents Adrift p 12
When Dinosaurs Ruled p 60

The Rest is History

During our recent past, the ice extended from the north and south to cover large areas of the Earth's surface. The climate was cooler, and animals such as the saber-toothed tiger and the woolly mammoth (below) were common. The first humans appeared about 40,000 years ago and hunted these animals.

Tree ferns

Sequoia

Gingko

Pine

First flying reptile

Ammonite

Earwig

Diplodocus

Pterodactyl

Swimming reptile

Poplar – early flowering plant

Early turtle

Woolly mammoth

Oak tree

Pterosaur

Triceratops

Woolly rhinoceros

Sabre-toothed tiger

Jurassic period
208-145 million years ago. The land split into smaller continents and the climate changed, bringing rain to the deserts. Dinosaurs thrived in huge forests of conifers and cycads. They became larger, more varied and increased in number, dominating the land.

Cretaceous period
145-65 million years ago. The climate became drier, conifers were fewer and the grasslands were formed. Dinosaurs began to die out and were replaced by birds and mammals. The first flowering plants brought color to the landscape.

Recent past

WHEN DINOSAURS RULED

Dinosaurs first appeared about 240 million years ago and ruled the Earth for 160 million years. The first ones were small and fast moving but, gradually, dinosaurs grew bigger. Towards the end of their reign, some spectacularly large herbivores such as Saltasaurus appeared. They were hunted by the king of the carnivorous dinosaurs – Tyrannosaurus rex. Then, 65 million years ago, the dinosaurs became extinct. Nobody knows why for certain.

LEFT: In 1842, British scientist Richard Owen declared that giant reptiles should be called Dinosauria, which means "terrible lizard." He then set about building dinosaur restorations, even going so far as to entertain his friends in the incomplete body of an Iguanodon!

BELOW: This map shows a range of different dinosaurs, positioned over the continents in which their remains have been found.

Struthiomimus
This dinosaur is called the ostrich mimic because of its resemblance to the modern ostrich. It had a small head, a long neck, and strong legs so that it could run very fast.

Diplodocus
Belonging to a group of plant-eating dinosaurs called sauropods, the massive Diplodocus reached over 89ft in length and had a 26ft long snake-like neck.

Iguanodon
In 1820, Mary Ann Mantell found a large tooth in some gravel. Her husband, an English doctor, believed it belonged to an enormous relative of the iguana, so he named it Iguanodon (meaning "iguana tooth"). It was the first dinosaur to be identified.

FANTASTIC FACTS

• The longest known dinosaur is Seismosaurus, at up to 170ft. Nicknamed the earthquake lizard, it was so heavy that the earth would have trembled as it passed.

• Stegosaurus was as large as an elephant, but its brain was only the size of a walnut.

• One marine dinosaur, Elasmosaurus, closely fits descriptions of the Loch Ness monster.

• The largest ever flying creature was a pterosaur, with a wingspan of 39ft.

Tyrannosaurus rex
This was the sort of creature nightmares are mad of. Its name means "tyrant lizard king," and it was the largest-ever carnivore. Strangely, its arms were so short that they didn't reach its mouth!

Brachiosaurus
This sauropod dinosaur was a giant! It weighed 50 tons and was as high as a four story building, able to reach leaves on the highest trees. A tall human would only come up to its knee.

Saltasaurus
Discovered in 1980, Saltasaurus was the first sauropod dinosaur to be found with armor plating. It had large body and a long neck, at the end of which was a tiny head.

Pterodactylus
Belonging to a group of flying reptiles called pterosaurs, Pterodactylus was a bat-like creature with leathery wings held out by its arms. It was quite small, with a wingspan of only 2ft. It used its huge, toothed beak to feed on dragonflies.

The first dinosaur eggs
Fossils of Protoceratops were first found in Mongolia in the 1920s, but equally exciting was the first-ever discovery of dinosaur eggs (above) alongside the remains. Each egg was 6in long and contained an embryo. The skeleton of Oviraptor (meaning "egg thief") was found nearby, leading scientists to believe that this reptile stole the eggs for food.

Tyrannosaurus rex

Stegosaurus

Velociraptor

Compsognathus

Diplodocus

Human

Putting the Pieces Together

There are so few dinosaur fossils that it is very rare to find a complete skeleton. Most skeletons on display are built using bones collected from different specimens. Dinosaurs evolved from the reptiles but, whereas reptiles hold their legs out to the side, dinosaurs hold theirs straight beneath their bodies, to support their weight (see right).

Skull
The shape tells us whether the dinosaur was a plant or a meat eater.

Hip
The shape and position shows whether the dinosaur walked on two or four legs.

Tail
A long tail was often used to counter-balance a long neck.

Legs
Their length and thickness indicate how heavy the dinosaurs was.

RIGHT: Before people knew about dinosaurs, they thought footprints like this were made by giants. Now scientists study these fossilized prints to find out more about the dinosaurs that made them, such as how heavy they were and how fast they ran.

Protoceratops
This was the first horn-faced dinosaur to be found. It had a bony frill around its face, and a beak that resembled that of a parrot. Other ceratop (horned-faced) dinosaurs were much larger, with frightening frills and spikes.

Tsintaosaurus
This dinosaur has caused much confusion in recent years. It was once thought to have a bony spike on its head, like a unicorn. But recent finds suggest that the spike in fact lay flat along the top of its head.

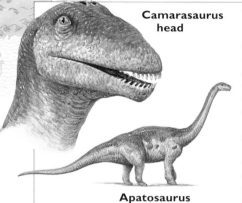

Camarasaurus head

Apatosaurus

THE BOGUS DINOSAUR

In America in the 1870s, there was a mad rush to find and name dinosaurs, which often led to some confusion. Fossil hunter Othniel Marsh named one dinosaur fossil Apatosaurus and another Brontosaurus, not realising they were the same animal. Then he built a model of Brontosaurus using the head of Camarasaurus! Things were not sorted out until 1979, when scientists agreed that the correct name should be Apatosaurus.

Tuojuangosaurus
This was a type of stegosaur, with two rows of bony plates running down its back. The plates were like prehistoric solar panels. When Tuojuangosaurus rested in the sun, blood flowing through the plates would absorb the sun's heat and spread warmth through the rest of the animal's body.

RIGHT: Finding dinosaur bones is the easy bit, but removing them from the rock is much harder! This palaeontologist (someone who studies fossils) is working in Dinosaur National Monument, using chisels and hammers to expose the fossilised bones. Once he has removed them, the bones will be encased in plaster before being taken to the laboratory for detailed study.

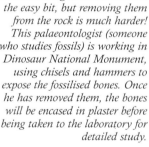
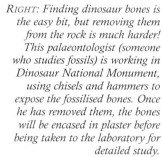

Muttaburrasaurus
Discovered in 1981, Muttaburrasaurus is one of the few dinosaurs to be found in Australia. It was similar to Iguanodon but had a bony lump on its snout which may have been used for display.

A Monument to Dinosaurs

One of the best places in the world to find dinosaur fossils is Green River Canyon in the American West. The site was discovered in 1908 by fossil collector Earl Douglass, since when more than 5,000 dinosaur bones have been found on the hillsides. In 1915 it became known as the Dinosaur National Monument. The cliff in which the remains have been found is formed from rock that was once a sand bank in a river. Dead dinosaurs floated down the river and became stuck on the sand bank, where their bodies were buried and fossilized.

Iguanodon

Protoceratops

From largest to smallest
The line up on the left shows the relative sizes of various dinosaurs and how they compare with a human. The largest dinosaurs, including the mighty Diplodocus, were all plant-eaters. The smallest was Compsognathus, which was the size of a chicken. Despite its size, Compsognathus was a vicious meat-eater, feeding on insects and lizards.

SEE ALSO
Life in the Past p 60
The First People p 66

WILDLIFE IN DANGER

More people, more industry and more farming all spell problems for wildlife. The natural world can't keep up with the rate at which humans are using resources. Nor can it cope with the vast quantities of pollutants that we pump into our rivers, seas and air. Plants and animals are becoming extinct at an alarming rate. Unless we do something about it, it is estimated that 25% of the world's species could become extinct within the next 50 years.

Polluting our water
People, industry and agriculture all produce waste materials. For many hundreds of years people have been dumping this waste into water (above) because it was quickly carried away out of sight. Nowadays, many rivers have become so polluted by the waste that their wildlife is under serious threat. The first animals to disappear are fish like salmon and trout that need very clean water. Rivers are easy to pollute, but it takes a lot of cleaning to make the water suitable for these fish again.

Forests Under Threat

Our forests are disappearing. Every week, millions of acres of forest are destroyed or damaged around the world. Ten thousand years ago, more than half of the world's land surface was covered in forest. Today, about 30% of the land is still tree-covered, but most of this is replanted forest – only a small fraction is original, primeval forest. These ancient forests survive in some of the most remote places on Earth, such as Papua New Guinea, Central Africa, Amazonia, northern Canada and Siberia. But even these forests are under threat from logging, mining, road and dam building, and industrial development.

ABOVE: Once a forest has been cleared the soil is soon washed away by the rain, so new plants can't grow.

A Delicate Balance

It may not seem important if the population of one animal suddenly falls, as there may be others to take its place. But all the plants and animals found in a habitat, such as the East African savannah shown below, live in a delicate balance which can easily be upset. If the numbers of antelope decrease, predators such as lions run out of food and begin to starve. If the lions die, the antelopes will increase in number because they are not kept in check by the lions. Too many antelope may mean the grasslands are overgrazed and eventually the antelope will starve.

BELOW: A simple food chain is easily upset if the population of one member decreases or goes up.

RIGHT: The map shows a range of endangered animals and plants and where they live. Lists of threatened species are drawn up by the World Conservation Union. There are about 150 mammals on the list and many more birds, fish, trees and other plants and animals.

Lion   **Antelope**   **Grass**

Red wolf
Found in Texas and Louisiana, this wolf is at risk through trapping and hunting.

Californian condor
A large bird of prey, under threat from food shortage and pesticides.

American crocodile
A large reptile, widely hunted for its skin and for sport.

Golden toad
Fast disappearing from the rainforests of Central America, but no one knows why.

Golden lion tamarin
This small monkey is threatened by the destruction of the Brazilian rainforests

Leatherback turtle
Found in tropical seas, where it gets trapped in fishing nets.

Chile pine
Also called the monkey puzzle tree, the Chile pine is suffering from forest clearance.

The Poacher's Game

In the last 25 years, the numbers of black rhinoceros have fallen from 30,000 to just 3,000 – all a result of poaching. The poacher is only after the horn which is used for medicines in the Far East, and as dagger handles in the Yemen. Although most poaching has now stopped, every year a few more animals are killed, including well-loved animals in the national parks of Kenya. The African Elephant has suffered a similar fate, but poaching has largely stopped now that the trade in ivory is illegal.

SAYING NO TO SOUVENIRS

Snakeskin handbag

Coral

Carved ivory

Conch shell

It is always tempting to buy holiday souvenirs. Tourist shops are full of attractive animal objects – brightly colored shells, natural sponges, bags made from animal skins and ornaments made from shells, bones and horns. But it is better to avoid these things. Unfortunately, the cheapest way for shops to get stock is to collect items from the wild. Local coral reefs may be picked clean of attractive shells, and animals may be killed just so they can decorate a home in a faraway place.

Antelope skin purse

Saving the Tiger

Today, there are many conservation schemes in operation, designed to increase the population of threatened species. One such is Project Tiger. Tigers once roamed forests throughout India, but deforestation and hunting caused their numbers to plummet from 40,000 in 1930 to just 1,800 by 1970. Project Tiger was launched in India in 1972 to save the tiger. Hunting was banned and new reserves were set up. By the early 1990s, the population had increased to 4,000. But a new threat loomed as hundreds of tigers were poached and slaughtered to make Chinese medicines. Even though most Chinese still believe that all parts of the tiger have medicinal powers, their government has finally agreed to help crack down on the illegal trade in tiger medicines.

SEE ALSO
Polluting Our Planet p 34
Tropical Rainforests p 42

Above: Bred in captivity, this young tiger cub will one day be released into the wild as part of Project Tiger's attempt to save this beautiful animal from extinction.

FANTASTIC FACTS

• Scientists estimate that between five and 15% of rainforest species could be extinct within the next 30 years – before many of them have even been identified!

• The rate of species extinction is now higher than it has ever been since the disappearance of the dinosaurs 65 million years ago.

• Every year, more than 200 million wild tropical fish are caught and taken to the USA for sale as aquarium fish.

Saimaa seal
The saimaa seal comes from Finland where it suffers from water pollution.

Siberian tiger
This central Asian tiger is widely hunted for its fur and medicinal powers.

Giant panda
Found in central China, the panda is at risk through loss of its favorite food – bamboo.

Sicilian fir
Found only in Sicily, where frequent forest fires and overgrazing have put it at risk.

Snow leopard
Loss of the wild sheep on which it preys threatens this cat.

Yangtze dolphin
A Chinese river dolphin that gets caught in fishing nets and collides with boats.

African violet
This common houseplant grows wild in Tanzania where it is suffering from loss of habitat.

Kouprey
Wild cattle from Indonesia, hunted for their horns.

Mountain gorilla
A great ape of central Africa, under threat from rainforest clearance.

Kakapo
Introduced stoats and rats threaten this New Zealand bird.

Sumatran rhinoceros
A rare species from South East Asia, under threat from hunting and deforestation.

Aye-aye
A nocturnal lemur, found only in the rainforests of Madagascar which are fast being destroyed.

Hairy-nosed wombat
This Australian marsupial is in fierce competition with rabbits and cattle for food.

Blue whale
Found in all the world's oceans, the blue whale was once widely hunted. Hunting has now been banned.

Return to the Wild

The orang utan is now only found on Borneo and Sumatra. In the past, young apes were taken from their mothers and sold as pets throughout South East Asia. But, when they grew up, they were totally unsuitable as pets so people locked them up in cages or simply abandoned them. There is now a special reserve in Sabah, Borneo, where rescued orang utans are taken to be introduced back into the jungle. The reserve is also now breeding orang utans, and numbers are happily increasing.

3
PEOPLE AND PLACES

If you travelled around the world, you would come across many different peoples and cultures. You would hear unfamiliar languages being spoken. People follow a variety of religions and political beliefs, wear different clothes, enjoy all sorts of foods and take pleasure from a wealth of music, writing and art. Differences may lead to conflict, but they also offer a chance for peoples to learn from one another. Since prehistoric times, human beings across the globe have all shared an interest in discovery and invention, in making beautiful objects, and in communication.

Farmers working in terraced paddy fields on an Indonesian rice plantation.

THE FIRST PEOPLE

How did people come to live on Earth? Scientists who try to solve this puzzle are called anthropologists, and they study fossils of prehistoric animals to work out how these creatures developed over millions of years. We now have evidence that humans share the same ancestors as some animal groups. Our family tree includes many creatures which are now extinct and some which are still living today, like the apes.

ABOVE: Mary Leakey hunted fossils of ape-like creatures and early humans in East Africa. With her husband, Louis Leakey, she made many important discoveries about our ancestors.

Clues from the past
The map (right) shows where the remains of human ancestors have been found. Anthropologists have unearthed fossils in Europe, Asia and Africa but no discoveries of early peoples have been made in the Americas.

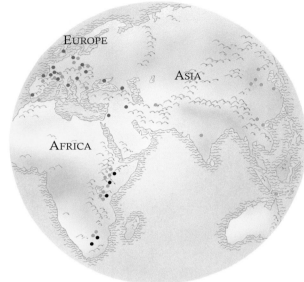

KEY

- Australopithecus africanus
- Homo habilis
- Homo erectus
- Homo sapiens neandertalensis (Neandertal person)

Australopithecus africanus ("African southern ape") was an ape-like creature which lived between three million and a million years ago. It walked upright at just over 3 feet tall and weighed 55–100lbs. Fossils have been found in South Africa, Ethiopia, Kenya and Tanzania.

Homo habilis ("handy person") was up to 5ft tall and weighed about 110lbs. It could probably make stone tools for hunting and simple shelters. Most remains have been found in East Africa, but fossils in South Africa and South East Asia may belong to the same group.

Lucy's Story

In 1974 two American fossil-hunters, Donald Johanson and Tom Gray, were looking for remains by the River Awash in Ethiopia. They found part of a three million-year-old skeleton. As they examined the bones, their radio was playing a pop song called "Lucy in the Sky with Diamonds," so they nicknamed their skeleton "Lucy." Lucy's scientific name was *Australopithecus afarensis*. She stood just over 3 feet tall. Although she walked upright on two legs (left), she probably spent a lot of time in the trees.

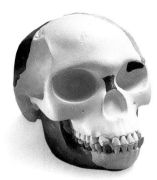

LEFT: In the 1900s people were looking for a "missing link" between apes and modern humans. They were delighted when a skull to fit this description was found in Sussex, England, in 1912, and they called it Piltdown Man. Forty-one years later, in 1953, the "fossil" was discovered to be a hoax. It was a modern skull with an ape's jawbone!

An adult chimp brain is about a quarter of the size of an adult human brain.

Clever chimps
Our closest relatives in the animal world are chimpanzees (below). These clever African apes make simple tools from twigs stripped of their leaves which they use to poke into termite nests and to collect wild honey. Chimps use stones to crack nuts and sometimes chew leaves to make a sponge for mopping up rainwater. They can walk upright, but mostly run about on all fours.

LEFT: This young chimp is using a twig to dig termites out of their nest.

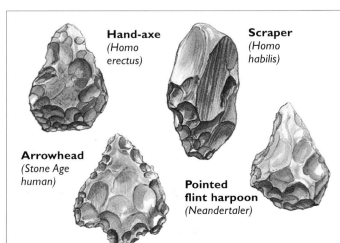

Hand-axe (*Homo erectus*)

Scraper (*Homo habilis*)

Arrowhead (*Stone Age human*)

Pointed flint harpoon (*Neandertaler*)

TOOL-MAKERS

Our early ancestors lacked the strength of the wild animals around them, but they were far more cunning. They learned to make weapons and tools of stone, bone and wood. The first tools were simple sticks and rocks. When modern humans developed about 40,000 years ago, they became expert at making flint tools (left) for scraping, cutting and boring.

Footprints in the ash
One day about 3.6 million years ago, a volcano erupted in East Africa, covering the ground with soft ash. Three ape-like creatures fled from the danger, leaving behind a trail of footprints. When the ash hardened into rock, the footprints (right) were perfectly preserved. They were discovered in 1976, at Laetoli, in Tanzania and are the earliest examples of our ancestors' footprints to have been found. The tracks show that early humans could move quickly and easily on two feet, leaving their hands free for other jobs.

SEE ALSO
Life in the Past p 58
Peoples of the World p 78

Homo erectus ("upright person") stood up to 6ft tall and weighed over 190lbs. This hunter could make tools from stone, wood and bone, use fire and build huts. Remains found in Africa, Europe and Asia date back to between 1.8 million and 200,000 years ago.

Neandertal people are named after a valley in Germany where their remains were found. They were stocky, with bigger brains than we have today. They mostly lived in Europe and the Middle East, from about 200,000 years ago. Neandertalers were an early version of *Homo sapiens* ("wise person," our modern group of humans).

Dignity for the Dead

Neandertalers lived through the bitter cold of the Ice Ages. Life in these conditions was difficult, dangerous and often short. Burials (right) were dignified occasions. Neandertal burial sites have been discovered from southwestern France to northern Iraq. In this picture of a Neandertal burial, a grave is being dug in the soft, wet earth inside a cave. The grave is lined with plants and wild flowers and the dead warrior is given food, weapons and tools for use in the after-life.

Mourners placed food and tools in the grave.

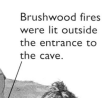

Bodies were laid in a sleeping position.

The grave was covered with stones and soil.

Neandertal people were cave-dwellers.

Brushwood fires were lit outside the entrance to the cave.

Prehistoric Hunters

Neandertal people died out between 40,000 and 35,000 years ago. The later Neandertalers lived alongside modern humans – some may have been killed by the newcomers. Neandertalers hunted prehistoric wild animals, such as the woolly mammoth (above) and the woolly rhino, to survive. Animal skins were scraped with flints and used to make clothes or tents, while the bones were kept to make needles and tools and the sinews made into thread or hunting snares.

FANTASTIC FACTS

• The world's oldest complete human skull was found in Kenya – it is around 2 million years old.

• Evidence that our ancestors have known how to use fire for at least 500,000 years was produced in 1929 when charred wood was found next to the remains of a *Homo erectus* skeleton.

• Recently, the bones of nearly 2,000 mammoths were excavated from a Stone Age rubbish dump in the Czech Republic.

ANCIENT CIVILIZATIONS

Great cities and splendid buildings, scientific inventions, arts, crafts and music, courts of law and fair government... over thousands of years peoples of the world have organized their societies and developed their cultural identities. Societies which have made important advances are called civilisations. By finding out about the great civilizations of the past, we can discover all sorts of marvels and objects of beauty – and some fascinating beliefs and ideas.

NORTH AMERICA
Extent of Mayan civilization

The Mayans of Mexico

The Mayans are a people of the Yucatán region of Mexico. Between about AD300 and 900 they built great ceremonial cities with pyramids, palaces and temples. No one lived in these cities – they were used only for sacred rituals and as administrative centres. The Mayan people lived in farming villages on the outskirts of their cities. They made beautiful stone carvings, paintings, jewellery and pottery. They also developed a system of writing, using little pictures.

Roman senate

The Mighty Roman Empire

In about 850BC a small settlement called Rome grew up in the hills of Central Italy. By AD250 this had become a huge city of over a million people, which ruled over all the lands from Britain to Morocco, from Spain to Jerusalem. A well-trained army, organized into legions of about 6,000 men, kept order over these lands. At first the Romans had kings, but they later became a republic. Each year they elected two leaders, or consuls and laws were passed by a senate (governing body). From AD27 onwards, the Romans were ruled by a powerful emperor.

EARLY WRITING

1

2

3

ABOVE: The Mayans sacrificed human beings to their gods, cutting out their hearts or drowning them. This was thought to be necessary for the survival of the world and was considered a great honor for the victims.

RIGHT: Our knowledge of ancient peoples is constantly being improved through archaeological finds. One of this century's most important discoveries was made in 1922, when the British archaeologist Howard Carter found the tomb of the young pharaoh, Tutankhamun, near Luxor in Egypt.

Sumerian scribes used a tool called a stylus to make wedge-shaped marks on wet clay tablets (1). The Egyptians developed a system of writing involving over 700 picture signs called hieroglyphs (2). Aztec and Mayan peoples used picture writing to keep details of their history and society. These records were collected into carefully folded books – called codices – made from bark paper (3).

Rome

Masked priest

Embalmer

Egyptians and the After-life

The ancient Egyptians believed that after death, people kept their bodies as they travelled to meet the gods. It was important that dead bodies were not damaged, so from about 3000BC onwards the Egyptians preserved them as "mummies" (right). First of all they pulled out the brain, then they put the innards in special containers called canopic jars. The rest of the body was dried out with a kind of salt and stuffed with cloth, clay or sawdust. The skin was rubbed with oils and wrapped in bandages before being shut inside coffin cases and placed in a tomb.

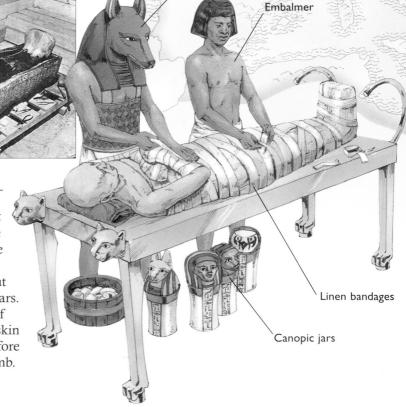

Linen bandages

Canopic jars

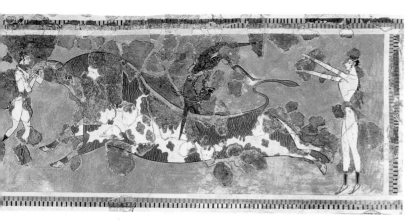

ABOVE: A fresco from the palace at Knossos. Young acrobats entertain a royal audience (and risk their lives) by vaulting over the horns of a sacred bull.

Island of Culture

The Minoan civilization, which takes its name from the legendary King Minos, flourished between 2000BC and 1450BC on the island of Crete in the Mediterranean Sea. The Minoans were great traders and skilled metal-workers, jewellers, potters, painters and weavers. They became wealthy, building fine cities and elaborate palaces. The palace at Knossos was excavated and restored at the beginning of the 20th century. In many of its rooms the walls are beautifully painted with scenes depicting Minoan life (left).

SEE ALSO
Traces of the Past p 70
Art and Culture p 86

BELOW: The tomb of Qin Shi Huangdi was guarded by a vast army of 7,500 warriors – made of terracotta (baked clay) or bronze. Each was beautifully modelled and was meant to protect the emperor after he died. This secret army was found by Chinese workers in 1974.

CHINA
Extent of Chinese empire by AD2

Classical Greece

About 2,800 years ago, Greece was made up of small independent states based on single cities or islands. These were not united, but all of them spoke the Greek language and worshipped the same gods. Every four years, representatives of all the states joined in an athletic and artistic festival held in honor of the gods at Olympia. Most Greek states had single rulers or kings. However, Athens was governed by a public assembly, a kind of government called democracy (or "rule by the people"). Ancient Greece produced great poets and playwrights, sculptors and artists. Greek philosophers and thinkers questioned the meaning of life and society, and still influence the way we see the world today.

China's First Empire

From about 2100BC onwards, many great civilizations arose in China. The ancient Chinese were brilliant inventors, traders, craft workers and artists. In 221BC they were united under the rule of a powerful emperor called Qin Shi Huangdi. He standardized the empire's currency, laws, weights and measures and written script. But his most lasting achievement was to strengthen the empire's northern defences into the Great Wall. Work continued after Qin Shi Huangdi's death and the wall reached its final extent during the Han dynasty.

Troy

Greek philosophers

Olympia
Athens
Knossos

Peoples of the Indus Valley

In the rich farmlands around the River Indus, great civilisations grew up which were at their most powerful between about 2500 and 2000BC. There were two beautifully planned cities called Harappa and Mohenjo-daro (right). These had fine houses, public and private baths, proper drains and large city granaries to store harvested crops. The Indus peoples made cotton textiles, jewellery of gold and precious stones, and little statues of copper and stone. They also used a form of picture-writing.

The city of Mohenjo-daro

Harappa

River Euphrates Ur

Giza

River Indus

Mohenjo-daro

River Nile

Luxor

FANTASTIC FACTS

• Pharaohs ruled over ancient Egypt for more than 2,500 years. In contrast, the Inca empire of South America survived for less than a century.

• The Minoan civilization was probably destroyed by a huge volcanic eruption on the nearby island of Santorini in 1450BC that sent 300ft high waves crashing over Crete.

• Aztecs believed the Sun needed human blood to rise every day, so they sacrificed 15,000 men a year to their Sun god.

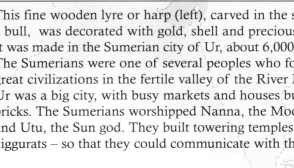

A Sumerian woman playing the lyre

The Sumerians

This fine wooden lyre or harp (left), carved in the shape of a bull, was decorated with gold, shell and precious stones. It was made in the Sumerian city of Ur, about 6,000 years ago. The Sumerians were one of several peoples who founded great civilizations in the fertile valley of the River Euphrates. Ur was a big city, with busy markets and houses built of clay bricks. The Sumerians worshipped Nanna, the Moon god and Utu, the Sun god. They built towering temples – called ziggurats – so that they could communicate with their gods.

TRACES OF THE PAST

Much of what we know today about ancient civilizations has been learned from the remains of spectacular buildings and monuments that were built many centuries ago. Archaeologists have discovered lost cities deep in the jungle or high in the mountains, and have unearthed great tombs and mysterious temples buried in the sand. From these they have pieced together a picture of how people lived and worshipped, the skills they had, and how they organized their society.

The Rose Red City

In the burning deserts to the northeast of the Red Sea, in Jordan, lie the remains of an ancient city called Petra. It was the capital of the Nabatean kingdom and was later ruled by the Romans. Petra was at its wealthiest about 2,000 years ago, when it controlled trading routes across Arabia. Petra was built in a valley surrounded by cliffs which acted as the city's natural defences. Many of Petra's buildings and tombs were cut from the pink sandstone cliffs (above), inspiring a poet to call it the "rose red city."

China's Great Wall

Work on the world's longest wall began over 2,300 years ago (right). It was built to protect the Chinese civilization from fierce warriors who might invade from the north. A roadway passed along the top of the wall, which was used by merchants as well as soldiers. Much of the Great Wall still stands today. The main part is over 2,145mi long, and sections branching off it make up the same distance again.

LEFT: Machu Picchu was an outpost of the Inca empire. The city remained undiscovered by the Spanish conquistadors but was found in 1911 by an American archaeologist called Hiram Bingham. As well as the ruins of houses and ceremonial buildings, many mummified bodies were found at the site.

Watchtowers were built into the Great Wall every several hundred feet.

The Lost City

In 1911, ruins of a long-lost city were discovered high in the Andes mountains, in Peru. They included beautifully constructed houses and temples. Machu Picchu (above) had been built by the Incas, a native American people who ruled a vast empire about 500 years ago. The Incas worshipped the Sun and made beautiful goods out of gold, silver and bronze. They were also expert potters, weavers and musicians, and had strict laws, as the ruins of a prison found at Machu Picchu reflect. The Inca emperors and nobles lived in great splendor until their lands were invaded by Spanish soldiers in the 1530s.

FANTASTIC FACTS

• Huge pictures of animals and 13,000 absolutely straight lines, etched across the deserts of Peru, were found in 1927. They were made by the Nazca people in around 200BC but no-one knows why or how.

• Each of the massive four-ton stones that make up the circle at Stonehenge was moved about 190mi from Wales to southern England.

Pyramids Around the World

Three vast pyramids tower over the desert sands at Giza, in Egypt. The biggest of these was built as a tomb for an Egyptian pharaoh called Khufu in about 2550BC. But the Egyptians were not the only people to build towering pyramids – remains of similar structures have been found in Central and South America, and in what is now Iraq, in a region once inhabited by the ancient Sumerians.

RIGHT: The Great Pyramid at Giza is the only one of the Seven Ancient Wonders of the World still standing.

Several chambers and passages were built inside the tomb, including the pharaoh's burial chamber.

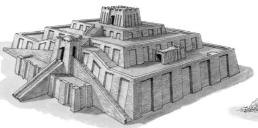

This reconstruction of a Sumerian pyramid, called a ziggurat, differs from an Egyptian pyramid in that it has steps and a square top. It was built in the ancient city of Ur in about 2100BC, in honour of Nanna, the Moon god.

Stepped pyramids were also built by the peoples of Central and South America. This one is at Chichén Itzá in Mexico. Built by the Mayans in about AD800, it served as a temple.

RIGHT: The Great Pyramid at Giza was built upwards and outwards from the center, with over 1,100 giant bricks added every working day.

A ramp of bricks and rubble was constructed for hauling huge blocks of stone to the top.

The blocks were transported on sledges pulled by oxen or men.

Workers used an escape route after the main passage had been sealed.

Stonehenge
This stone circle was constructed about 4,800 years ago.

The Parthenon
Standing on a rock high above Athens, this temple was built by the ancient Greeks and dedicated to the goddess Athene.

SEE ALSO
Conquerors & Crusaders p 72
Amazing Buildings p 88

NORTH AMERICA

EUROPE

Stonehenge

ASIA

Mesa Verde
The Anasazi Native Americans built cliff dwellings, cut into the canyon at this site.

Rome · Athens · Ur · Petra

Mesa Verde

Giza · Abu Simbel

Angkor Wat
This is the biggest religious site in the world. A huge temple to the Hindu god Vishnu, it was built by the Kmers in the 1100s in what is now Cambodia.

Chichén Itzá

Angkor Wat

AFRICA

Chan Chan
Citizens of Chan Chan lived in adobe mud brick houses built within large enclosures. The city fell into ruins in around AD1470.

Chan Chan

Machu Picchu

Abu Simbel
The colossal statues erected at the temple of Rameses II, pharaoh of ancient Egypt, are over 3,000 years old.

Great Zimbabwe

AUSTRALASIA

Aboriginal art
Australian Aborigines made drawings on smoke-blackened bark or painted with ochre on the walls of their caves.

SOUTH AMERICA

Great Zimbabwe
Remains of this walled city were found in southern Africa. The site was first settled about 1,000 years ago.

BELOW: The maze of corridors and animal pens that were built under the floor of the arena can now be explored by tourists visiting the Colosseum.

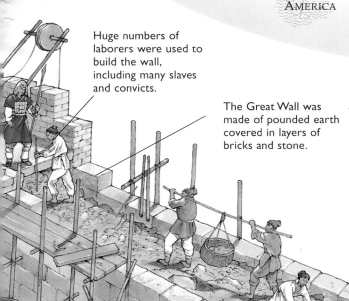

Huge numbers of laborers were used to build the wall, including many slaves and convicts.

The Great Wall was made of pounded earth covered in layers of bricks and stone.

The Arena of Death

The Colosseum (right) is a vast arena in the center of Rome, built to hold over 50,000 spectators. Completed in about AD80, it was used by the Roman emperors to stage spectacular and gruesome shows. In this way the emperors hoped to stay popular with the public who liked to watch people die fighting wild animals or battling as gladiators. The ring could even be flooded for mock sea-battles.

CONQUERORS AND CRUSADERS

Throughout history, rulers have tried to conquer other lands, to control trade, gain wealth and extend their influence. They have built up great empires. Whole peoples have been on the move, looking for new territories which they can settle. Some invaders have brought peace and justice, while others have murdered and looted, and enslaved the peoples they conquered. Many wars have been fought over religious beliefs. In the Middle Ages, Christians called their "holy" wars "crusades," while the Muslims called theirs "jihads."

Viking invaders
The Vikings were seafarers from Scandinavia. Armed with battle axes and swords, they attacked shipping and coastal towns in foreign lands.

NORTH AMERICA

EUROPE

Ruthless Romans
Roman armies were the deadliest in the ancient world. The soldiers wore helmets and armor and carried fearsome short swords and spears.

AFRICA

Armed Aztecs
The Aztecs conquered large parts of Mexico before being defeated by Spanish soldiers in the 1520s. Aztec warriors were armed with wooden clubs and spears edged with razor-sharp stone.

Zulu attack
Zulu warriors, armed with spears and clubs, fought in regiments called impis. They conquered large areas of southern Africa in the early 1800s. In 1879, during the Zulu Wars, they defeated British soldiers at Isandhlwana.

SOUTH AMERICA

The Conquering Hero

Alexander the Great (right) is said to have been one of the most brilliant soldiers and wisest rulers the world has ever seen. He was born in Macedonia, in northern Greece, in 356BC. Aged only 22, this young man led a Greek army into Asia and defeated the superpower of his day, Persia. Alexander went on to bring vast areas of the Middle East under his rule, and founded a great city called Alexandria in Egypt. His empire soon stretched all the way to India. He died of fever at Babylon in 323BC, leaving no heirs, and his kingdom was divided between his generals.

Hannibal and his Elephants

Few people managed to defeat the mighty Roman empire. But a general from Carthage in North Africa succeeded time after time. Hannibal was born in 247BC. When he was only nine, his father made him swear to be an enemy of Rome. Hannibal went on to lead a great army through Spain and France into Italy. That meant climbing the snowy mountain passes of the Alps – together with the war elephants which he used in battle (below)! After 14 years of winning battles across Italy, Hannibal returned to Africa where he was defeated by the Romans in 202BC.

ABOVE: Hannibal crossed the Alps with 40 elephants and an army of 30,000 men. Many of the soldiers and animals died on the way.

Genghis, Horseman of the Plains

Temujin, born in 1162, was only 13 when he took command of the fierce Mongol armies of eastern Asia. His horsemen swept across the grassy plains and deserts of Central Asia, and the steppes and forests of Russia. They were feared far and wide. From 1206 onwards Temujin became known by the title "Genghis Khan," which means "mighty ruler." His armies invaded northern China, and by his death in 1227, he had created an empire which stretched from the Black Sea to the Pacific Ocean.

Controlling with Castles

During the Middle Ages, invaders built great castles to control the lands they conquered. The first castle-builders were the Normans, descendants of Viking warriors who had settled in northern France. They conquered large areas of Europe. Their first castles were wooden towers built on high mounds, surrounded by defensive ditches. Later, castles had thick stone walls, such as the crusader castle, Krak des Chevaliers, in Syria (right). Stone castles were attacked with great catapults and battering rams. When big cannons came into use, castles were less easy to defend.

Mongols on the move
Mongol warriors overran Asia from the 1100s to the 1500s. They rode on horseback and were armed with swords as well as powerful bows and arrows.

ASIA

Macedonian tactics
The ancient Macedonians fought in a tight formation called a phalanx. They attacked using long stabbing spears and defended themselves by locking their shields together.

Battling Huns
Between 430 and 450AD, these Asian warriors and their allies defeated countless armies from China to Italy. Their terrifying leader, Attila, was known as the "Scourge of God."

Samurai soldiers
The Samurai were the knights of medieval Japan. They observed a strict code of honor. Samurai were skilful archers, but also fought with spears and some of the sharpest swords ever made.

LEFT: A French manuscript illustration showing the defeat of the Muslim leader Saladin and his Turkish troops by Christian soldiers in 1192.

Two Centuries of Holy Wars

The Crusades were a series of wars fought between 1096 and 1291. On the one side were Christian knights from all over Europe. On the other side were Saracens – Muslim warriors who included Turks, Arabs and Kurds. They fought to control the lands of the Near East, which were holy to both Christians and Muslims. The behavior of both sides was often brutal and far from holy. However there was one leader admired by all, a Muslim called Saladin, who lived from 1137–1193.

SEE ALSO
Voyages of Discovery p 74
World Religions p 82

FANTASTIC FACTS

• Between 850AD and 1700 it is estimated that 50,000 castles were built across Europe – that's an average of one castle completed every six days!

• The tradition of Japan's medieval knights lasted for several centuries – in 1871 there were still 400,000 Samurai in Japan.

• Babur, the first ruler of the mighty Mughal empire in India, began a brilliant career as an army leader when he was just 14 years old.

Condemned to a Life of Slavery

Many conquerors, from the Romans to the Arabs, enslaved the peoples they conquered, taking away their freedom and forcing them to work hard for no money. One of the cruellest periods of slavery began in the 1500s, when Europeans seized people from West Africa. The Africans were packed into ships and taken across the Atlantic Ocean. Many died on the way and the survivors were sold into slavery in the Americas. Although transatlantic slavery was abolished in the mid-19th century, Arabian slave traders were still operating in East Africa in the 1890s (above).

VOYAGES OF DISCOVERY

Long before air transport made exploration so easy, many brave travellers set out in ships and on foot to discover distant, unknown lands. They made contact with the peoples who lived there, brought back exotic foods and fabrics, plundered gold and precious gems, and recorded the strange plants and animals they came across. In about AD1000 Vikings crossed the Atlantic, but it was another 500 years before people succeeded in circumnavigating (sailing around) the globe, during an era called the "Age of Discovery."

ABOVE: This 15th century map of the world is a copy of one made by an Egyptian geographer called Ptolemy, who died in AD168. At the time it was drawn, people had to guess the shape of most countries.

Opening Up North America

In 1804, Meriwether Lewis and William Clark (above) set out to explore the unknown lands to the west of the Missouri River, in North America. With the help of native American guides, they crossed the whole continent, reaching the Pacific Ocean after 18 months of wandering.

ABOVE: Columbus is greeted by the natives of San Salvador, in the Caribbean, who are eager to trade with their visitors from the east.

Discovering a New World

Christopher Columbus was an Italian seafarer who took service with the Spanish king and queen. In 1492 he set sail across the Atlantic with three tiny ships, trying to find a new route to southern Asia. When he finally reached what he thought was Cathay (as China was once known), he had, in fact, landed in the Caribbean. His discovery of the Americas made Spain very rich, but spelt disaster for the Native American peoples. The Europeans slaughtered many of them and stole their lands and gold.

Viking Exploration

The Vikings were warriors from Scandinavia who sailed far and wide in their finely-built longboats in search of land and riches. When Eric the Red was banished from Norway for murdering someone, he sailed west and founded a colony in Greenland in the year 986. His son Leif Ericsson sailed further still, and became the first European to set foot in America, in about AD1000.

ABOVE: In this 19th century painting, Leif Ericsson is depicted spying land for the first time since setting sail from Greenland. He landed first in Labrador, then visited Baffin Island and Newfoundland. He named the latter Vinland after the wild grapes he found there.

Around the Globe

Ferdinand Magellan was a Portuguese navigator who, like Columbus, entered the service of the king of Spain. In 1519 he sailed with five ships to South America in search of a southern route to the Pacific. He found a route through a narrow sea passage that was later named after him – the Strait of Magellan – but he was killed in the Philippines. His crew brought his ship safely back to Spain, becoming the first people to sail around the world.

PACIFIC OCEAN

CARIBBEAN

SOUTH AMERICA

Strait of Magellan

BELOW: After a journey fraught with mutiny, starvation and shipwreck, Magellan and 40 of his men were butchered in the Philippines when they got involved in a quarrel between local chiefs.

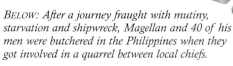

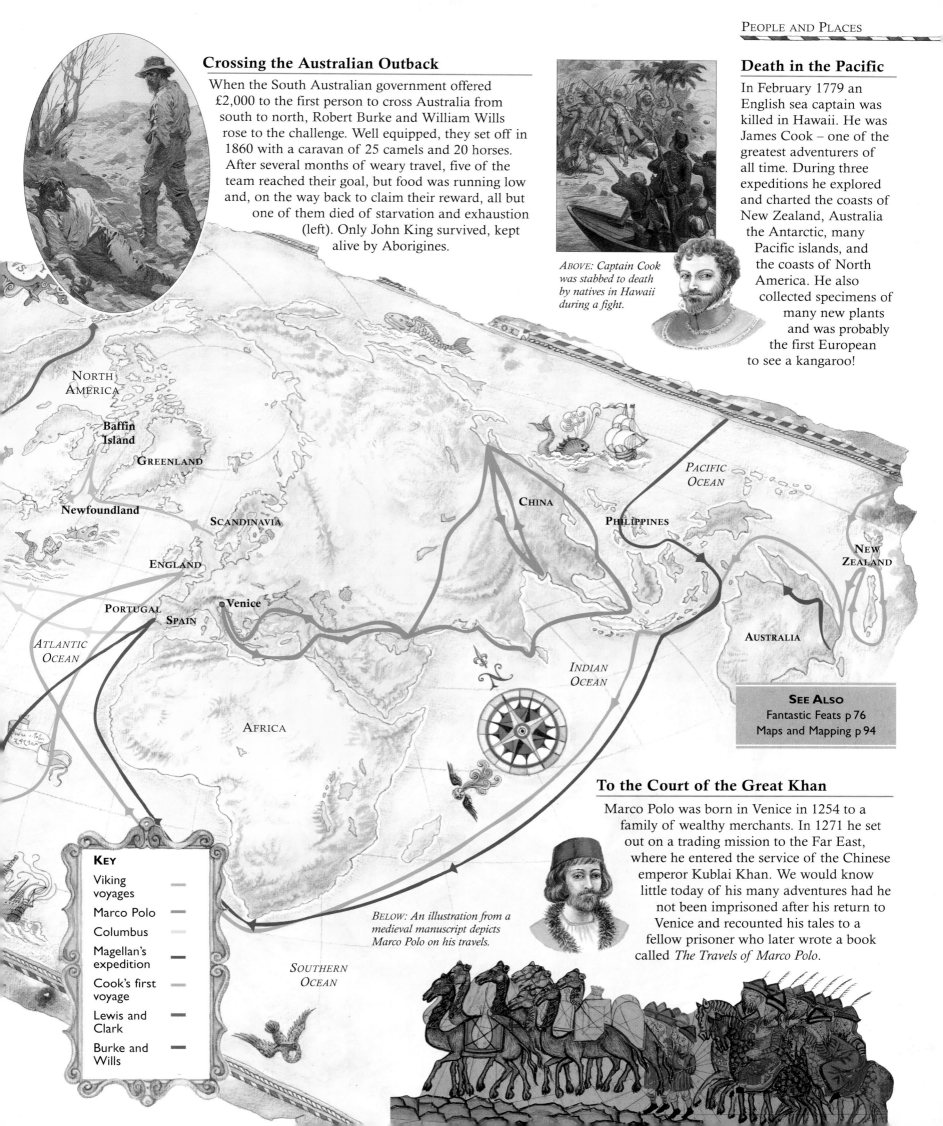

Crossing the Australian Outback

When the South Australian government offered £2,000 to the first person to cross Australia from south to north, Robert Burke and William Wills rose to the challenge. Well equipped, they set off in 1860 with a caravan of 25 camels and 20 horses. After several months of weary travel, five of the team reached their goal, but food was running low and, on the way back to claim their reward, all but one of them died of starvation and exhaustion (left). Only John King survived, kept alive by Aborigines.

Death in the Pacific

In February 1779 an English sea captain was killed in Hawaii. He was James Cook — one of the greatest adventurers of all time. During three expeditions he explored and charted the coasts of New Zealand, Australia the Antarctic, many Pacific islands, and the coasts of North America. He also collected specimens of many new plants and was probably the first European to see a kangaroo!

ABOVE: Captain Cook was stabbed to death by natives in Hawaii during a fight.

SEE ALSO
Fantastic Feats p 76
Maps and Mapping p 94

To the Court of the Great Khan

Marco Polo was born in Venice in 1254 to a family of wealthy merchants. In 1271 he set out on a trading mission to the Far East, where he entered the service of the Chinese emperor Kublai Khan. We would know little today of his many adventures had he not been imprisoned after his return to Venice and recounted his tales to a fellow prisoner who later wrote a book called *The Travels of Marco Polo*.

BELOW: An illustration from a medieval manuscript depicts Marco Polo on his travels.

NORTH AMERICA

Baffin Island

GREENLAND

Newfoundland

SCANDINAVIA

ENGLAND

Venice

PORTUGAL
SPAIN

ATLANTIC OCEAN

AFRICA

CHINA

PHILIPPINES

PACIFIC OCEAN

NEW ZEALAND

AUSTRALIA

INDIAN OCEAN

SOUTHERN OCEAN

KEY

Viking voyages	—
Marco Polo	—
Columbus	—
Magellan's expedition	—
Cook's first voyage	—
Lewis and Clark	—
Burke and Wills	—

FANTASTIC FEATS

People have always pushed themselves to the limits. The 20th century in particular has witnessed some incredible examples of human endeavor. From ocean depths to mountain peaks, from the frozen poles to the skies, men and women have used their skills of endurance in all kinds of hostile environments. Sometimes these feats have helped us to make scientific discoveries. Sometimes they have put new technologies to the test. And sometimes they have been done just for the thrill.

Woman above the clouds

In 1932, an American called Amelia Earhart became the first woman to fly solo across the Atlantic Ocean. Her other aviation feats included a single-handed flight across the United States. In 1937, Earhart began a round-the-world flight but after completing two-thirds of the journey her aircraft mysteriously disappeared over the Pacific Ocean.

Atlantic First

On 14 June 1919 two British airmen, Captain John Alcock and Lieutenant Arthur Whitten Brown, took off from St John's in Newfoundland, Canada, in a Vickers Vimy military aircraft. Their target was to be the first to fly non-stop across the Atlantic Ocean, a distance of 1,890mi. They met foul weather and had to fly low, climbing out of the cockpit to knock heavy ice off the plane. After 16 hours and 27 minutes they landed in County Galway, Ireland, to receive a heroes' welcome. And, in recognition of their skill and determination, the two men were knighted by King George V. Tragically, Alcock died in a flying accident six months later but the record he had set with Brown stood for eight years until the American aviator Charles Lindbergh flew the same distance single-handed.

CANADA
Alcock and Brown's route
IRELAND

ABOVE: The record-breaking Vickers Vimy was a biplane powered by twin Rolls-Royce Eagle VIII engines and equipped with long-range fuel tanks.

FANTASTIC FACTS

• The greatest ocean descent was achieved in 1960 by two crew members of a US naval expedition. Inside a special vessel, they reached a depth of 35,815ft.

• Swimming the English Channel *once* is a feat of endurance – the first successful *triple* crossing was made by American Jon Erikson in 1981.

• The first human being to go into space was Russian cosmonaut Yuri Gagarin. His historic orbit lasted 118 minutes.

On Top of the World?

American explorer Robert Peary made many Arctic expeditions in his attempt to reach the North Pole. Finally, in 1908, he set off from Greenland with a team of 50 Inuit (people who live in the Arctic) and 250 dogs. Most of the team was sent back during the hazardous journey but on April 5, 1909 Peary claimed to have reached his goal, recording the event in a photograph (right). In spite of this evidence, some experts remain to be convinced that Peary ever reached the Pole.

The Moon Walkers

For centuries, flying to the Moon was just a dream. Then, with the advent of the space age in the 1950s, it became an attainable goal and on July 21, 1969 a United States space mission, Apollo 11, landed on the Moon. Astronauts Neil Armstrong and Edwin "Buzz" Aldrin became the first human beings ever to cross its rocky, empty surface. Without the effects of wind or water erosion, their footprints (left) should stay visible for 10 million years!

Peak of Achievement

The highest and meanest mountain in the world is Everest, towering to 29,030ft above sea level. It poses the ultimate challenge to every mountaineer and has claimed many lives. The first men to reach the summit were a New Zealander called Edmund Hillary and Tenzing Norgay, a Sherpa from the Himalayan foothills, on May 29, 1953 (right). Since this historic feat, over 400 climbers have made it to the top, some of them without the use of bottled oxygen.

Tiptoeing across Niagara

One of the greatest showmen of all times was a Frenchman called Charles Blondin (1824–97). He trained as an acrobat and in 1859 he crossed a tightrope high above the Niagara Falls, on the border between the United States and Canada. Determined not to be outdone by his challengers, Blondin repeated the feat in more and more hair-raising ways – blindfolded, backwards, on stilts, on a unicycle and even pushing another man in a wheelbarrow!

Scott's doomed expedition

While Amundsen was celebrating his Antarctic triumph, a British team of explorers, led by Robert Falcon Scott (below), was also heading for the South Pole. Pulling their own sleds, they arrived, exhausted, in January 1912 – only to find that they had been beaten to their goal by Amundsen. Tragically, none of Scott's team survived the journey back.

ABOVE: In 1947 a wooden raft, the "Kon-Tiki," was wrecked on a remote Pacific reef. The crew, led by a Norwegian called Thor Heyerdahl, all survived. It was the end of a 4,600mi-journey that Heyerdahl was making from Peru to support his theory that ancient Peruvians had sailed to the Pacific islands hundreds of years earlier.

Antarctic Adventure

The first person ever to stand at the South Pole was a Norwegian called Roald Amundsen. As a teenager he was fascinated by accounts of the attempts to find a "northwest passage," the route round the icy Arctic waters of North America to the Pacific Ocean, and they inspired him to devote his life to polar exploration. In June 1910, after careful preparations, Amundsen set out across the Antarctic. With a team of four men dressed in thick fur clothing, and sleds pulled by dogs (right), Amundsen made fast progress across the ice and arrived at the South Pole on December 14, 1911.

South Pole

ANTARCTICA

Key
- - - Amundsen's route
- - - Scott's route

SEE ALSO
The Earth in Space p 10
Worlds of Ice p 18

77

PEOPLES OF THE WORLD

Our planet is home to a huge variety of peoples. All human beings share the same basic needs, such as food, housing, education and communication. Many also share a love of art, craft, science and technology. But there are differences, too, and a rich pattern of cultures has grown up, to match the full range of climate and conditions. People may speak different languages, grow various crops, live in alternative types of home, or worship different gods.

Arctic Dwellers

The Inuit live in the icy Arctic lands of Greenland, Canada and Russia. Traditionally they lived by hunting and fishing (left), but today, some work in fish-processing factories or in the Arctic oil industry. Many families now live in modern villages, and are more likely to travel by snowmobile than dog sled.

GREENLAND

CANADA

Fishing for a living
A Cree Native American uses a small traditionally built boat for fishing.

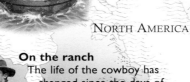

Native Navajo
This woman is preparing a leather hide. Many Native Americans live by making and selling craft items.

Festival sounds
The bagpipes are the national instrument of Scotland. They are played at many festivals and ceremonies.

Alpine nations
Skiing is a popular sport for people living in Alpine countries and for tourists visiting the region.

NORTH AMERICA

On the ranch
The life of the cowboy has changed since the days of the Wild West, but many Americans still work as farmers, ranching cattle or growing wheat on the huge prairies.

The American dream
The American way of life has been influenced by settlers from Europe, Africa and Asia, who have all become American citizens. They are united in their love of sports, such as football.

Spanish steps
Fancy footwork, clicking castanets and acoustic guitars are all part of the flamenco – music and dance that started with the Gypsies of southern Spain.

EUROPE

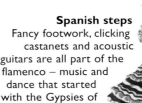

Tradition in the city
This Berber water seller offers cool drinks to passers by on the streets of Marrakech in Morocco.

Life in the tropics
Many Caribbean people are of African descent. A large number grow tropical crops, such as sugar cane, bananas or cotton.

SAHARA DESERT

Unchanging lifestyles
The Himba are one of the few groups of Herero peoples to have kept to their traditions in Namibia. They live by herding cattle.

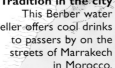

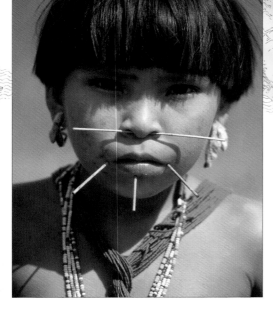

LEFT: Many Yanomami still wear necklaces and pierce their bodies in the traditional style.

Mountain existence
Native Americans who speak the Quechua language live in the high mountains of the Andes, growing maize and potatoes.

BRAZIL

Surviving in the Forest

Indigenous people are the original inhabitants of a particular region. The Native American Yanomami (above) are an indigenous people who live in the mountainous forests of Venezuela and Brazil. Since the arrival of Europeans in the Americas 500 years ago, many indigenous peoples have suffered terrible persecution and disease. But the Yanomami have held on to many of their old traditions, farming crops such as the plantain and hunting and fishing in the forest.

SOUTH AMERICA

Cowboy cult
Gauchos first became famous in the 1800s as the wild cowboys of the Pampas, an area of grassland that covers 20% of Argentina.

FANTASTIC FACTS

• Over 10,000 different languages and dialects are spoken around the world today.

• Standard Chinese is the world's most wide-spread language and is spoken by 750 million people.

• Papua New Guinea has a population of just 4 million, yet more than 800 different languages are spoken on the island.

AFRICA

Ancient Africans
The San people of the Kalahari desert are the descendents of some of the first peoples to live in southern Africa.

A Travelling Life

The Berber peoples are the original inhabitants of North Africa. They live in the dry, mountainous lands of North Africa and in the empty wastes of the Sahara Desert. Some Berbers grow crops, while others raise livestock, travelling with their herds to new pastures for part of the year. Berber peoples, such as the Tuareg (left), are always on the move, trading across the Sahara.

HOME SWEET HOME

High, boat-shaped roofs are a feature of traditional timber houses in Sulawesi, Indonesia (1). The Marsh Arabs, or Ma'dan, live in the wetlands of southern Iraq and build houses from rushes on low, artificial islands (2). Thatched huts built of mud may still be seen in many parts of tropical Africa. They are cool, cheap to build, and are often beautifully crafted (3).

Cossack culture
The Cossacks live on the grasslands or steppes of eastern Europe. They became famous for their skilled horsemanship and wild dances.

RUSSIAN FEDERATION

National workforce
This factory worker belongs to one of the many different ethnic groups living in the world's biggest country – the Russian Federation.

ASIA

China's majority
The Han people make up about 90% of the vast Chinese population.

SEE ALSO
Farming Around the World p 80
Countries of the World p 96

Warriors and Farmers

Papua New Guinea includes many remote areas of forest and mountain, and is home to a large variety of cultures. The Genalei people live in the eastern highlands of the country, and at feasts and ceremonies some warriors still wear beautiful feathers, body paint, masks of mud or ornaments of shell and bone (above). Many people in Papua New Guinea farm root crops, such as sweet potatoes, and raise pigs, while others work on the coffee and tea plantations.

Eastern farmers
The Mongol people live on the grassy steppes and desert fringes of the Far East. They are expert horse riders who herd sheep.

Spiritual dance
An Indian woman performs an ancient dance to the sound of drums. The dance tells the story of Hindu gods and demons.

Dress code
This Iranian woman wears a shawl over her head as a mark of her faith. Iran is governed acording to Islamic law.

Heavy duty
Sumo wrestlers aim to topple each other in this traditional Japanese sport.

Staple grains
Rice is the most important food crop for the peoples of Southeast Asia. This rice farmer is from Vietnam.

PAPUA NEW GUINEA

Pacific Peoples

The Chuuk Islands are a maze of coral reefs and atolls, making up part of the Federated States of Micronesia. This woodcarver (below) from the region is working on a canoe – boat-building skills like this have been important to the Micronesian and Polynesian peoples for thousands of years, helping them to settle over vast areas of the Pacific Ocean. Today, islanders live by fishing, farming, mining or by working in tourism.

Masai on the Move

The Masai people (above) are mostly cattle herders, whose dusty grasslands stretch across the borders of Kenya and Tanzania in East Africa. Modern methods of cattle farming, tourism and development have all affected the Masai way of life. But some traditions have remained the same, such as the fact that young men, wearing cloaks and hair braided with ochre, live in separate camps, and women wear elaborate necklaces and earrings.

Minority communities
Aboriginal peoples have lived in Australia for over 40,000 years. Today they are greatly outnumbered by settlers from other parts of the world.

AUSTRALASIA

Island inhabitants
The Maoris, descendants of Polynesian seafarers, have lived in New Zealand for nearly a thousand years. They have retained many of their ancient traditions.

FARMING AROUND THE WORLD

Around the world, 240,000 babies are born every day. The world's human population is expanding at an incredible pace, and we all depend on food to survive. Farmers raise poultry to give us eggs and meat, and also breed animals such as pigs, cattle, sheep and goats. "Staple" crops – rice, maize, wheat, millet and sorghum – give us basic foods, such as bread. Other crops, including fruits, nuts and vegetables, provide important vitamins to keep us healthy. Much of the world's natural grassland, such as the prairies of North America, is now used for growing crops or cattle-ranching. Intensive farming methods can cause problems over time and many farmers are changing their farming methods to take better care of the Earth.

BELOW: The map shows the most important crops that are grown around the world and where farm animals are reared. Large sections of the globe remain uncultivated because they are too dry, too cold, too mountainous or too remote.

KEY

- Cultivated land
- Coffee
- Tea
- Cotton
- Tropical fruits
- Temperate fruits
- Sugar cane
- Wheat
- Maize
- Rice
- Sheep
- Cattle

Fruit of the Vine

Grapes have been grown for wine-making for thousands of years. Since Roman times France has produced some of the world's finest red and white wines. The famous "pinot noir" variety of grape is grown and harvested on vineyards in Burgundy, central France (right). Other grape-producing regions around the world include Germany and Central Europe, Mediterranean countries, California, Chile, South Africa and Australia.

Rice Work

Channels allow water to flow from one paddy field to another.

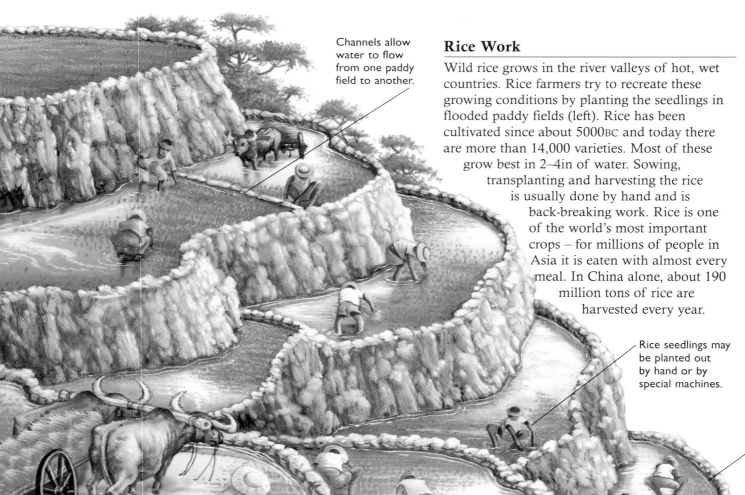

Wild rice grows in the river valleys of hot, wet countries. Rice farmers try to recreate these growing conditions by planting the seedlings in flooded paddy fields (left). Rice has been cultivated since about 5000BC and today there are more than 14,000 varieties. Most of these grow best in 2–4in of water. Sowing, transplanting and harvesting the rice is usually done by hand and is back-breaking work. Rice is one of the world's most important crops – for millions of people in Asia it is eaten with almost every meal. In China alone, about 190 million tons of rice are harvested every year.

Rice seedlings may be planted out by hand or by special machines.

The hillside is terraced so that the water does not run away down its slopes.

FANTASTIC FACTS

- The world's largest cattle ranch is in Australia. It is 18,540mi² in area – about three-quarters the size of the Netherlands.

- In New Zealand, sheep outnumber people by fifteen to one.

- The biggest turkey on record, a bird by the name of Tyson, weighed in at a staggering 39kg.

- The global fish catch is about 76 million tons per year and Japan accounts for 13% of this catch.

Fields of gold
The prairies of the United States and Canada are sometimes called the world's "bread basket," because they produce so much wheat. Combine-harvesters cross the wide fields to reap and thresh the grain (left).

Harvesting the Sea

Fish and shellfish are a valuable source of healthy food, but modern fishing methods have brought stocks of some species to dangerously low levels. This has happened in the North Sea and off the coast of Newfoundland. Sometimes, the numbers of fish have been reduced by pollution of the water. For example, oil slicks have prevented flying fish breeding off the coast of Barbados. In some places, the size of a catch is now strictly limited, because there are too many fishing boats, like this British trawler (right), going after too few fish. One solution to the shortage is to breed more fish, such as salmon and carp, on special fish farms. Today, fish farming supplies 13% of the world catch.

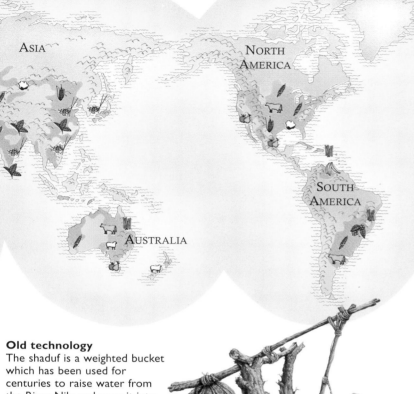

SEE ALSO
Climate and Weather p 30
Great Disasters p 90

Old technology
The shaduf is a weighted bucket which has been used for centuries to raise water from the River Nile and pour it into channels in the fields along the banks. This means that riverside crops can be easily watered. Modern irrigation methods, including electric pumps, hoses and sprinklers, now make it possible to turn deserts green.

Cattle Country

Vast numbers of beef cattle are raised on the estancias, or ranches, in the Pampas, an area of grassland in Argentina (above). Beef exports are an important source of income for Argentina. Brazil has also become a large exporter of beef. A vast area of cleared rainforest is now grassland where cattle graze. Much of the beef is sold to multinational burger companies.

Bananas grow upwards in tight clusters. Each cluster is called a hand.

Have a Banana!

Banana plants originally came from Southeast Asia, but today they are grown in many tropical lands, including Africa, Central America and the Caribbean. There are many different kinds of the fruit, some with yellow skins, others with reddish or green skins. Yellow bananas (right) are picked before they are ripe, and exported in refrigerated ships to be eaten as a sweet fruit. In many tropical countries large green bananas, called plantains, are cooked and eaten in the same way as vegetables.

Farming to Survive

Small farmers in many parts of the world grow just enough food to feed their own family – this is called "subsistence" farming. Others harvest enough to sell extra produce at market. Large farms (above) produce "cash crops" which are sold for exports. This can make the farm owner rich, but the farm workers may not always share in the profits.

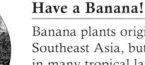

The bananas will be washed with insecticide before they are packed.

81

WORLD RELIGIONS

From the earliest times people have searched for ways of understanding the great mysteries of life and death. Was the world created by God? Do we live on after death? Is our fate decided by the stars or by good and evil spirits? Over the ages, some people have worshipped nature spirits, while some have come to believe in many gods and others in a single God. Some people are atheists, and see all religion as superstition.

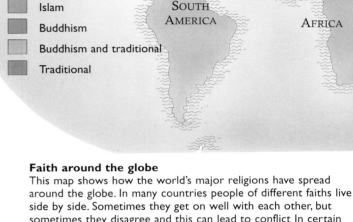

KEY

- Christianity
- Hinduism
- Judaism
- Islam
- Buddhism
- Buddhism and traditional
- Traditional

NORTH AMERICA
EUROPE
SOUTH AMERICA
AFRICA

LEFT: Hindu pilgrims come to the city of Varanasi to bathe in the River Ganges. Bodies are cremated beside the sacred river.

LEFT: Shiva, the god of renewal through destruction, is specially revered by many Hindus.

Death and Rebirth

Hinduism developed in India about 4,000 years ago. Hindus believe in a supreme spirit or force called Brahman. This divine spirit takes many forms, represented by gods and goddesses. The most important are Brahma, Vishnu and Shiva. Hindus believe that all living things are reborn after they die, and that past deeds affect life in the present, a belief called "karma." Holy scriptures include the Veda, a collection of ancient hymns. Today, over 732 million people around the world follow the Hindu faith.

Faith around the globe

This map shows how the world's major religions have spread around the globe. In many countries people of different faiths live side by side. Sometimes they get on well with each other, but sometimes they disagree and this can lead to conflict In certain regions, such as in parts of Africa, indigenous peoples have followed the traditional beliefs of their ancestors for centuries. However, many of them are now converting to other faiths.

LEFT: Symbols of Judaism include the branched candlestick, or menorah, the prayer shawl and skull cap worn by Jewish men, and the Torah, or holy scriptures.

A sacred city

Jerusalem, in Israel (below), is a holy city for Jews, Christians and Muslims. Sadly this has resulted in conflict throughout its history. It is a beautiful city which includes many sacred sites. Jews gather for prayers at the Western Wall (right). Muslims worship at the golden Dome of the Rock. Christian pilgrims visit the Church of the Holy Sepulcher and the Via Dolorosa.

The Chosen People

Jews believe that there is a single God, and that they are his chosen people. Their aim is follow God's Law, which was revealed to Moses on Mount Sinai over 3,000 years ago after he led the Israelites out of Egypt. One of the most important Jewish festivals is the Passover which celebrates this exodus (escape) from slavery in Egypt. Jewish beliefs are summed up in the first five books of the Bible – the Torah. Today, the faith of Judaism has over 17 million followers across the globe. Jews worship in synagogues and receive their religious teaching from rabbis. Jewish children often learn Hebrew, the ancient language of the Jews.

The Teachings of the Buddha

"Buddha" means "enlightened one," and is the name given to Siddhartha Guatama, an Indian prince who was born in about 563BC. At the age of 30, he gave up all his wealth to lead a simple life of meditation and teaching. Like the Hindus, Buddhists believe in karma (the way that past actions affect the present) and in rebirth. They shun attachment to material things and to the self, which they believe only brings misery. The Buddhist aim is to break away from the chain of karma by getting rid of all desires and achieving a spiritual state known as nirvana. There are about 315 million Buddhists worldwide.

LEFT: Many Buddhist temples contain statues of the Buddha meditating. Worshippers sometimes leave offerings of flowers and incense.

ASIA

AUSTRALASIA

ABOVE: Buddhist priests, called lamas, blow long horns at a ceremony in Tibet's Ta Gong monastery. As in most religions, different beliefs and rites have grown up within the Buddhist faith. The Tibetan spiritual leader is known as the Dalai Lama.

RIGHT: Holy Week falls in the week before Easter and commemorates the trial and death of Jesus. In Spain, Holy Week is marked with processions through the street. Traditionally some of the people wear tall hoods to show they are sorry for their sins.

BELOW: Christians eat bread and drink wine at Holy Communion to remember the Last Supper shared by Jesus and his disciples (followers) before he was put to death.

The Five Pillars of Islam

Islam has five central duties, or "pillars of faith." Followers of Islam, called Muslims, must believe that there is a single God, called Allah, and that his prophet is Muhammad. Secondly, Muslims must pray to Allah five times a day. Thirdly, they must help the poor by giving alms (donations to charity). Fourthly, they must fast, or take no food, in daylight hours during the month of Ramadan. The fifth pillar of Islam is pilgrimage, and the holiest journey of all is to Mecca, where Muhammad was born in AD570. There are 1,025 million Muslims worldwide.

RIGHT: Thousands of Muslims gather at the shrine, or Ka'ba, of the Great Mosque in Mecca, Saudi Arabia. Pilgrims must walk around the shrine seven times.

Christian Beliefs and Followers

Christians place their faith in Jesus, a Jew born about 2,000 years ago, whom they believe to be the Christ or Son of God. He was put to death on the cross, but Christians believe Jesus rose from the dead and ascended to heaven. Christ's teachings are written in the New Testament of the Bible, and Christians aim to spread his message to others and to love and care for their fellow human beings. Christianity has 1,833 million followers worldwide.

SEE ALSO
Festivals & Celebrations p 84
Amazing Buildings p 88

FANTASTIC FACTS

• Until the 1960s, an order of Christian monks, known as the Trappists, spent their lives in continual silence. Now they are allowed to talk during the day.

• The tallest minaret (tower) of any mosque is 660 feet high. It is at the Great King Hassan II Mosque in Morocco and was built in 1993. It is topped by a laser beam.

The Dome of the Rock dominates Jerusalem's skyline.

FESTIVALS AND CELEBRATIONS

People celebrate all kinds of events with special fairs, festivals and feasts. Some of these are personal, such as birthdays or weddings, while others have serious religious meanings, such as Easter for Christians or Guru Nanuk's birthday for Sikhs. Festivals may mark the passing of the seasons or may recall important events in the history of a nation. Some celebrations may honor the arts or major sporting events – and others are held purely for fun.

Traditional Christmas
The Germans first used real fir trees to decorate their houses at Christmas, the festival marking the birth of Jesus. This custom spread around other Christian countries in the 1800s. In the days before electricity and fairy lights, candles were fixed on to the branches to give a magical light.

RIGHT: Horses thunder around the track at Calgary, in the Canadian province of Alberta. The big "stampede," held each July, has become a major tourist attraction.

BELOW: The map shows a small selection of the many festivals held around the world throughout the year. Every country has a unique way of celebrating its history and culture, but all the different events have a sense of fun in common.

NORTH AMERICA

Halloween
Originally a pagan festival, October 31 is now the night when American children go "trick or treating."

Fourth of July
Each summer, the USA marks its freedom from Britain on Independence Day. There are many parties, parades and firework displays.

Inti Rayma
This festival of the Sun is held in June each year near Cuzco, Peru. It celebrates the traditions of the Inca people.

SOUTH AMERICA

Farming Festivals

The Calgary Stampede celebrates the skills of the "rodeo" or cattle round-up (above). Rodeos are popular on the prairies of Canada and the United States. They include exhibitions of horse-riding and roping steers (bullocks). Competitors also try to stay mounted on a wild, unbroken pony, or "bucking bronco" and spectators wear the costume of the pioneering days of the 1800s. Cattle fairs in South America also honor the traditional cowboys of Argentina, the "gauchos." Other types of farming and ranching have their own festivals, with sheep-shearing competitions and even pig races. Some of the world's oldest festivals celebrate sowing and harvesting crops.

Riot of Color

The first carnivals took place in the Middle Ages. They were the last chance to feast and be merry before the Christian period of fasting, called Lent. Carnivals are still celebrated all over the world, from the Fastnacht of Germany to the Mardi Gras of New Orleans. One of the most spectacular is held each year in Rio de Janeiro, Brazil. This five day carnival is a colorful celebration of the samba, a swaying, rhythmic dance which is very popular. Tens of thousands of people take to the streets, dancing in spectacular, glittering costumes (left). Elaborately decorated floats drive through the crowds.

FANTASTIC FACTS

● In the Hindu temples of Bali, an island in Indonesia, at least 35,000 important religious festivals are held each year!

● Many Christian festivals are held on saints' days. Worldwide, there are more than 2,000 officially "registered" saints – so that's a lot of festivals!

● The world's largest ever gathering at a festival took place at Allahabad in India on February 6, 1989 when an estimated 15 million people assembled for the Hindu festival of Kumbh Mela.

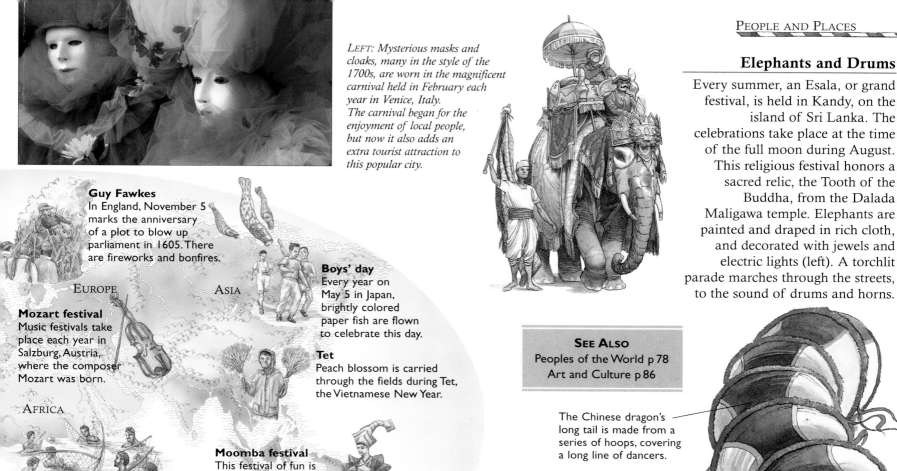

LEFT: Mysterious masks and cloaks, many in the style of the 1700s, are worn in the magnificent carnival held in February each year in Venice, Italy. The carnival began for the enjoyment of local people, but now it also adds an extra tourist attraction to this popular city.

Guy Fawkes
In England, November 5 marks the anniversary of a plot to blow up parliament in 1605. There are fireworks and bonfires.

EUROPE

ASIA

Mozart festival
Music festivals take place each year in Salzburg, Austria, where the composer Mozart was born.

Boys' day
Every year on May 5 in Japan, brightly colored paper fish are flown to celebrate this day.

Tet
Peach blossom is carried through the fields during Tet, the Vietnamese New Year.

AFRICA

Fishing festival
The winner of the Argungu festival, held every March in Nigeria, is the fisherman who can catch the largest perch. The competition is accompanied by dancing and cultural displays.

Moomba festival
This festival of fun is held every summer in Melbourne, Australia.

AUSTRALIA

Elephants and Drums

Every summer, an Esala, or grand festival, is held in Kandy, on the island of Sri Lanka. The celebrations take place at the time of the full moon during August. This religious festival honors a sacred relic, the Tooth of the Buddha, from the Dalada Maligawa temple. Elephants are painted and draped in rich cloth, and decorated with jewels and electric lights (left). A torchlit parade marches through the streets, to the sound of drums and horns.

SEE ALSO
Peoples of the World p 78
Art and Culture p 86

The Chinese dragon's long tail is made from a series of hoops, covering a long line of dancers.

Dragons are often red and gold as these are thought to be lucky colors.

Major Milestones

The Pende people of southern Zaïre, in Central Africa, welcome boys into adult life with a special ceremony (above). The Pende wear beautiful costumes and masks for many of their rituals and dances. Festivals which celebrate someone's progress through life are called "rites of passage." They may include religious landmarks, such as a Christian's First Communion, or a Jewish boy's Bar Mitzvah. They may mark weddings or sad occasions too, like funerals.

Swaying tassels help the dragon to move as if it is really alive.

Dragon Dancers

The Chinese Spring Festival, or New Year, is celebrated each year on a day between January 21 and February 20. It is welcomed wherever Chinese people have settled in the world, from San Francisco to London. A "dragon" (left) is a familiar part of the festivities, bobbing and weaving through the streets. Firecrackers explode, to scare away evil spirits. Families gather together to hold special feasts. They place new year greetings around their front doors.

ART AND CULTURE

People have always taken delight in painting colors and shapes, in making beautiful objects and in playing music. The arts have often had a religious purpose – many fine buildings and works of sculpture were made to honor gods. Some poems and stories record the history of rulers and nations. And art can also be simply an expression of feelings or a celebration of beauty.

A Rebirth of the Arts

As the Middle Ages drew to an end, in the 1400s, Italy saw a great revival of learning and scholarship, of science, mathematics, and philosophy and in the classical art of ancient Greece and Rome. This period is known as the Renaissance (meaning "rebirth"). The Renaissance produced great artists, sculptors and architects, including Botticelli (1445–1510), Michelangelo (1475–1564) and Leonardo da Vinci (1452–1519).

Painters of Light

In 1872 a French painter called Claude Monet called one of his pictures *Impression, Sunrise*. Soon the name "Impressionist" was being given to paintings in a similar style. The Impressionist artists rejected the formal studio paintings of their day. They painted outside and tried to capture the effects of sunlight and shadow. Impressionist paintings remain among the best-loved works of art ever produced.

RIGHT: In his Le Moulin de la Galette *(1876) Auguste Renoir creates the impression of dappled afternoon sunshine and the movement of dancing couples.*

LEFT: There are classical influences in Botticelli's La Primavera (Spring) *painted in around 1477.*

FAR LEFT: Classical sculpture was studied and copied during the Renaissance.

Grand opera
In the 19th century German composers, such as Richard Wagner, became famous for their dramatic operatic works.

Celtic design
This neck band, or torque, crafted from gold and silver, was probably made for a Celtic prince or princess in Europe over 2,000 years ago.

Greek decoration
The ancient Greeks painted legendary warriors and athletic dancers on pottery wine vessels like this one.

GERMANY   EUROPE   TURKEY

GREECE

Metal work
A fine bronze head, made in the West African kingdom of Benin 600 years ago.

Rock paintings
Pictures painted on rocks in the Sahara desert over many thousands of years show animals, hunters and herders.

Art of the mask
Masks are used in traditional festivals and rituals all over the world. This one is from Zambia.

AFRICA

Drums of Africa
Drums have always played an essential part in African music. Other musical styles, such as jazz, can trace their origins back to African rhythms.

Russian ballet
Russia has a long tradition of ballet, dating back to the days of the composer Peter Tchaikovsky (1840–93). Famous ballet companies include the Kirov and the Bolshoi.

Christian icons
Medieval Russian and Greek artists of the Orthodox Church made religious paintings called icons. Many were inlaid with gold and jewels.

RUSSIA

Status symbol
Bronze – an alloy of lead, copper and tin – was used extensively in China from 1500BC to 200BC. Bronze objects, like this horse, were made for the Chinese nobility.

Mughal manuscripts
Painting at the courts of India's Mughal emperors was delicate and finely detailed.

ASIA

INDIA

The sitar
This beautiful stringed instrument is played alongside drums in classical Indian music.

Imperial style
Turkish flower-patterned plates were made about 450 years ago in the days of the Ottoman empire.

BELOW: Henry Moore's Reclining Figure: Angles *was sculpted in bronze in 1979.*

The Shapes of Modern Times

In the 20th century, many artists and sculptors turned away from art which represents landscapes or the human body as they are seen by the eye. Instead, many turned to "abstract" interpretations – experimenting in color, form and shape. The British sculptor Henry Moore (1898–1986) worked with marble, bronze and stone, producing highly stylised human figures.

Japanese Style

The decorative arts have always been very important in Japan – from the simple black brush-strokes of Zen painting to the elaborate lacquer-ware and richly woven textiles of the 16th century. During the 17th, 18th and 19th centuries, popular art styles included screen paintings and wood-block prints. Among Japan's greatest artists were Utamaro (1753–1806) and Hokusai (1760–1849). Their works had a significant influence on European painters in the late 1880s.

ABOVE: A Japanese wood block print made by the artist Kuniyoshi (1797–1861).

ABOVE: Roy Lichtenstein's Whaam! (1963) uses comic strip as art. As on a printed page, the picture is formed from small colored dots (see left).

The World of Pop Art

In the 1950s some artists in North America and Europe began to have fun by making paintings and prints from everyday images. They felt that art should be more relevant to contemporary life. The work of artists such as Andy Warhol (1926–87), and Roy Lichtenstein (born 1923) ranges from images of soup cans, comic strips and magazine advertisements to pin-ups of film and pop stars.

Japanese drama
Male actors in traditional costume play the parts of both men and women in colorful Kabuki dramas, which date back 400 years.

JAPAN

Chinese porcelain
Delicate blue and white vases were made in China nearly 600 years ago, during the period of rule by the Ming emperors.

CHINA

Hindu carvings
Sculptors carved stone friezes for a Hindu temple on the Indonesian island of Java about 1,100 years ago.

Haida handicrafts
This beautifully-crafted mask was made by the Haida Native American people in the 1800s.

NORTH AMERICA

Paintings on the Plains
Paintings on rawhide show the battles between Native American peoples of the Great Plains and the white colonists during the 1800s.

Toltec pillars
These stone figures guarded a temple of the Toltec people built in Mexico 1,000 years ago.

Golden god
About 600 years ago the Mixtec people were the finest craft workers in Central America. This gold ornament shows their god of death.

MEXICO

Panama vase
Colorful vases shaped like birds and animals were made in Panama over 1,000 years ago.

SOUTH AMERICA

Mochica pottery
A man's portrait makes up this spouted vase, made by the Mochica people of the Andes between 100BC and AD700.

PERU

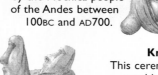

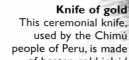

Knife of gold
This ceremonial knife, used by the Chimú people of Peru, is made of beaten gold inlaid with turquoise.

Cave paintings
The people, animals and plants represented in Aboriginal cave paintings are ancestors from the mythical "dreamtime."

AUSTRALIA

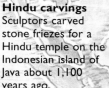

Didgeridoo tunes
Made from a wooden tube about 1m long that has been hollowed out by termites, the didgeridoo is a traditional Aboriginal instrument with a low, undulating tone.

AUSTRALASIA

Easter statues
Huge stone statues were put up by the inhabitants of Easter Island in the Pacific 900 years ago.

NEW ZEALAND

Jade jewellery
Maoris wore neck pendants to bring good luck and ward off evil spirits. This one is made of jade mined from the South Island.

Sounds of the Andes
The hollow tubes of the "pan-pipes" or *rondadors* have been played by the Native American peoples of the Andes for centuries.

FANTASTIC FACTS

• The world's most expensive painting sold at auction is Vincent van Gogh's *Portrait of Dr Gachet*, which was sold for $82,500,000 in New York in 1990.

• The world's biggest art gallery is the Hermitage in St Petersburg, Russia. Visitors would have to walk 24km to see all of its 3 million works of art!

• The *Mona Lisa*, painted by Leonardo da Vinci in 1507, was first purchased by King Francis I of France for his bathroom in 1517.

SEE ALSO
World Religions p 82
Amazing Buildings p 88

AMAZING BUILDINGS

Architects and engineers are always changing the appearance of our towns and cities, raising fine buildings of wood, stone and brick, or of steel, concrete and glass. Many cities have famous historical landmarks, such as places of worship, splendid palaces, theatres and museums. In the last century, advances in technology made it possible to build impressive new skyscrapers, which were first seen in American cities such as Chicago and New York. Today, gleaming high-rise towers are found in most large cities around the world.

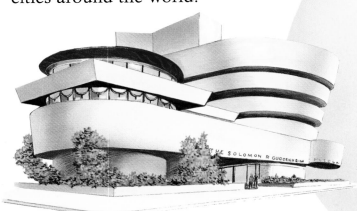

Spiral Showcase

The Guggenheim Museum in New York City (above) is a gallery of modern art, and was the last great building to be designed by the famous American architect Frank Lloyd Wright. It was built between 1943 and 1959. To view the paintings inside, visitors walk around a continuous spiral ramp, so they do not have to pass in and out of different rooms. The curving shapes of the concrete outer walls follow the same spiral design.

Buried in Beauty

Many people believe that the Taj Mahal (below), near Agra, India, is the most beautiful tomb in the world. It is built of gleaming white marble and is inlaid wth precious stones. It was constructed between 1632 and 1653 by the Mughal emperor of India, Shah Jehan, in memory of his wife, Mumtaz Mahal.

LEFT: The Mughal emperors were Muslims and Islamic influences can be seen in many of the buildings they commissioned. As the Islamic faith does not allow the representation of humans or animals in art, abstract floral designs and inscriptions from the Qur'an (the Muslim holy book) were used to decorate the walls of the Taj Mahal. The domes, minarets (towers), and pointed arches are all typical of Islamic architecture.

Statue of Liberty
Given to the USA by France in 1886, this 350ft tall monument greets visitors approaching New York City by ship.

NORTH AMERICA

The Capitol
The US Capitol building was built in Washington, DC between 1851 and 1863. Its dome is 223ft high.

New York

Washington, DC

Lloyd's of London
This high-tech steel and glass office block, built in 1986, has an "inside out" construction with all its pipes and working parts on the exterior.

Leaning tower
Pisa's famous bell tower was built over 800 years ago. It now tilts 16ft to one side.

EUROPE

London

Versailles   **Pisa**

Royal residence
The palace of Versailles, just outside Paris in France, was built for King Louis XIV between 1670 and 1700.

AFRICA

Djenné

SOUTH AMERICA

Christ of Rio
A stone figure of Christ tops Sugar Loaf Mountain overlooking Rio de Janeiro in Brazil. It was unveiled in 1931 and stands 125ft tall.

Rio de Janeiro

Mud mosque
Built in the same way as traditional African homes south of the Sahara, the Great Mosque in Djenné, Mali, is the world's largest dried mud building.

FANTASTIC FACTS

• The world's biggest dome, 680ft in diameter, tops the world's largest indoor sports arena, the Louisiana Superdome, in New Orleans, LA.

• The world's highest apartment building is part of the John Hancock Center in Chicago, IL. It has 100 storys and is 1,127ft high.

• The oldest known free-standing building on the globe is a temple on the island of Malta. It dates back to 3250BC, some 350 years before the earliest Egyptian pyramid.

BUILDING STYLES

The great public buildings of ancient Greece and Rome, like the Parthenon in Athens (1), have had a lasting influence on world architecture. A major revival of classical architecture began during the Renaissance. The Gothic style, with its slender spires and arched windows, dominated medieval Europe. Chartres Cathedral in France (2) is a fine example of a Gothic church. The modernist movement in 20th-century art was reflected in functional, geometric buildings. The Swiss architect Le Corbusier designed houses, such as his Villa Savoye in France (3), to be "machines for living in."

Sacred and secret

The world's largest palace is the Imperial Palace in Beijing, China (above). It is called "The Forbidden City," because in the days of the Chinese emperors, ordinary people were not allowed behind its high red walls. The palace is surrounded by wide moats, and dates back to the 1400s.

Decorative Domes

The skyline of the Russian capital city, Moscow, includes the towers of an old fortress, the Kremlin, and the onion-shaped domes of many Orthodox churches. The small cathedral of St Basil on Red Square (right) was built between 1555 and 1560. Its colorful domes are a distinctive feature.

Tibetan palace

A thousand steps lead up to the Potala, in the city of Lhasa. The palace was rebuilt for Tibet's religious leader, the Dalai Lama, in 1642.

ASIA

Lhasa

Amritsar

Himeji

Himeji Castle

Completed in 1608, this fine castle on Japan's Honshu island is heavily fortified, with massive stone foundations.

Golden domes

The dazzling Golden Temple stands in the Indian city of Amritsar. It is the world's holiest Sikh temple.

Yogyakarta

Borobudur Temple

This impressive 8th century temple in Yogyakarta on the Indonesian island of Java is adorned with 504 shrines of seated Buddhas.

AUSTRALASIA

Culture shock

The Sydney Opera House (above) rises from the waters of Sydney Harbor, Australia. It was designed by the Danish architect Jørn Utzon and built between 1959 and 1973. At first, the daring building provoked much argument, but soon it became one of the world's best-loved landmarks.

CN Tower
(1975)
Toronto,
Canada:
1,814ft

World Trade Center
(1973) New York City:
1,362ft

Sears Tower
(1974) Chicago:
1,453ft

SEE ALSO
Ancient Civilisations p 68
Peoples of the World p 78

Petronas Towers
(1996) Kuala Lumpur, Malaysia:
1,483ft

Chrysler Building
(1930) New York City: 1,046ft

Empire State Building
(1931) New York City:
1,250ft

Eiffel Tower
(1889) Paris, France: 984ft

Higher and Higher!

Until the late 19th century, the world's tallest structures were towers, such as the Eiffel Tower in Paris. Then in 1871 most of Chicago was destroyed by fire. American architects redesigned the city, building homes and offices upwards. By the 1880s, it was possible to raise steel-framed skyscrapers, served by high-speed lifts. By 1931, New York City's Empire State Building was the world's highest, but this was overtaken in 1973 by the World Trade Center. In 1996, the twin Petronas Towers in Kuala Lumpur, Malaysia, broke all world records, at 1,483ft. Radio towers and masts soared even higher.

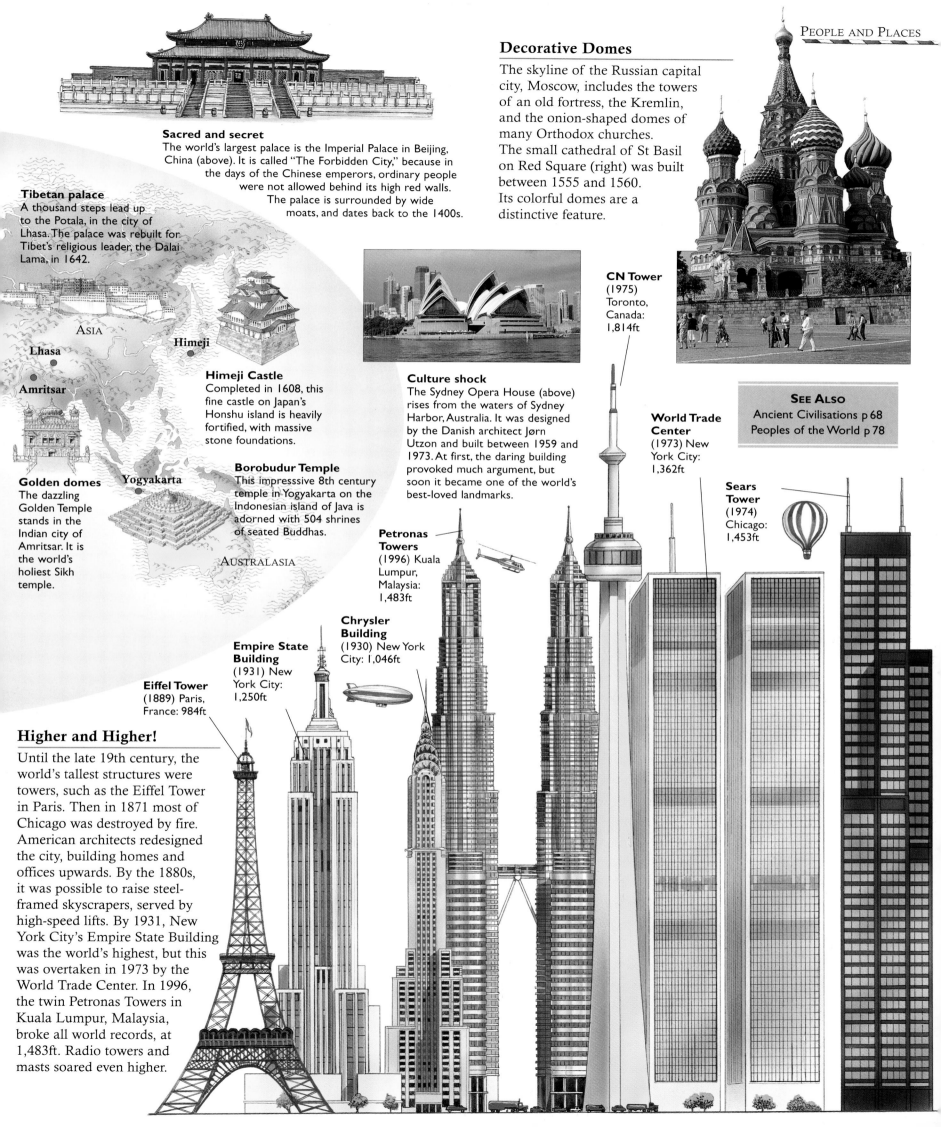

GREAT DISASTERS

Wherever people have settled over the globe, they have had to contend with the forces of nature. Volcanoes erupt, the earth quakes, floods cover the land, winds blow down trees and buildings, huge waves batter coasts, droughts kill crops and cause famine, and diseases sweep across continents. In addition, there are human accidents to deal with – from industrial catastrophes and pollution to shipwrecks and air disasters. But, in spite of these risks, people are safer and live longer today than they ever have before!

NORTH AMERICA

Crude Oil Catastrophes

In 1978 the *Amoco Cadiz* smashed into the rocky shoreline at Finistère, northwestern France (above). Over 223,000 tons of thick crude oil spewed into the sea, causing major ecological damage to coastal areas of France and Britain. The cost of cleaning up an oil slick is enormous: after the *Exxon Valdez* ran into rocks off the Alaskan coast in 1989, 6,000 people and $643 million were needed for the clean-up operation.

BELOW: A dust storm approaches the town of Springfield, Missouri, in May 1937. The storm, which swept across the area in the afternoon, created total darkness for about half an hour.

Volcanoes
In 1980, Mount St Helens in Washington State, did not so much erupt, as blow apart. It exploded in a cloud of ash and smoke and after the blast the height of the mountain was reduced by 400m.

USA

ATLANTIC OCEAN

Tornadoes
These small, powerful, twisting storms last only an hour or so. But they cause intense damage in certain areas, such as "Tornado Alley" across the southern states where 700 tornadoes strike each year.

PACIFIC OCEAN

Avalanches and landslides
Rocks, snow, ice and mud – or a combination of all four – can tumble down a mountainside, in an all-engulfing avalanche or roaring landslide. The 20th century's worst avalanche engulfed the town of Huarás in Peru in 1941, killing 5,000 people.

PERU

Misery in the Midwest

Poor farming methods take moisture and nutrients from the soil, leaving it dry, dusty and easily blown away. In the 1930s droughts and high winds turned the midwest region into a giant Dust Bowl (above). This natural catastrophe coincided with the misery caused by a recession in the US economy. Thousands of families faced starvation and were forced to leave their homes.

SOUTH AMERICA

Hurricane Horror

Hurricanes start out at sea, whipping up 80ft high waves. They affect the Caribbean and the coastline of the USA between June and November. If a hurricane comes ashore it can cause loss of life and serious damage to property. The cost of repairing the destruction caused by hurricane Andrew as it swept through Florida and Texas in August 1992 (right) has been estimated at $22 thousand million.

CHILE

Earthquakes
The force of an earthquake is measured by seismologists using the Richter scale. In 1960 the city of Concepción, in Chile, suffered one of the most powerful earthquakes ever recorded (8.5 on the Richter scale). Nearly 6,000 people died.

LEFT: An apartment resident looks out from the shattered remains of his home in Miami, destroyed by hurricane Andrew.

FANTASTIC FACTS

● In 1902 Mont Pelée erupted near St Pierre on the Caribbean island of Martinique, killing all 26,000 inhabitants except one – a prisoner who survived in his cell!

● Only a fraction of all volcanic eruptions are on land, about 99% occur under the sea.

● In 1981 a tornado struck the Italian port of Ancona, lifting a carriage 50ft into the air and setting it down again 300ft away without even waking the sleeping baby!

Nuclear Nightmare

In 1986 the nuclear reactor at the Chernobyl power station (right) in the Ukraine blew up and spread radioactive substances as far as Western Europe. Although only 31 people died in the event, scientists estimate that the effects of radiation in the environment will claim 100,000 lives over the next 30 years.

Earth-shaking Facts

The world's most earthquake-prone areas are in the "Ring of Fire" around the Pacific Ocean. Japan is regularly affected by tremors and in 1995 Kobe, the country's fifth largest city, was hit by a massive earthquake (right). Sections of the city's elevated roads collapsed into buckled wrecks and thousands of people died in the rubble.

ABOVE: Traffic in the city of Kobe at a standstill in the aftermath of the 1995 earthquake that measured 7.2 on the Richter scale.

ASIA

Epidemics
Diseases caused by germs spread rapidly in dirty, unhygienic places. The Black Death, a form of bubonic plague, killed more than 140 million people across Europe and Asia in the 14th century, almost a quarter of the worldwide population.

UKRAINE

EUROPE

Tsunamis
Undersea earthquakes, especially in the Pacific, set off huge waves, called tsunamis, which sweep away coastal towns and ruin farmland with salty floodwater.

JAPAN

Big Bang

In 1883, the Indonesian volcanic island of Krakatoa erupted, hurling 16mi^3 of rock into the sea (left). The blast was heard 3,000mi away. Volcanic dust spread throughout the world and shock waves from the explosion were felt even in California, 9,000mi from the island. No one died from the eruption itself, but 36,000 people were killed by tsunamis that followed.

AFRICA

BANGLADESH

Floods
Winter snows melt in high mountains and swell rivers with spring floods. Low-lying countries such as Bangladesh can be devastated by flooding, and the disease and famine that follow.

ETHIOPIA

Famine
Farm crops can be ruined by drought, flood, disease and insect plagues. In the 1970s–80s, some two million people starved as a result of famine, worsened by disease and war, in Ethiopia.

INDONESIA

INDIAN OCEAN

Cyclones
On Christmas Day in 1974, the city of Darwin in northern Australia was almost flattened by a cyclone (tropical storm). Thanks to warnings and storm protection, few people died.

SEE ALSO
Earthquakes & Volcanoes p 14
Climate & Weather p 30

AUSTRALIA

The Perilous Seas

At midnight on April 15, 1912, the "unsinkable" *Titanic*, the world's largest ocean liner, struck an iceberg near Newfoundland in the Atlantic Ocean on its maiden voyage (left). As passengers danced in the liner's ballroom, the order was given to abandon ship but, without enough lifeboats, less than 700 of the 2,200 people on board escaped with their lives. The *Titanic* was the first vessel to send out the new international distress call, SOS, which had been adopted earlier in the year but rescue ships were unable to reach the stricken liner quickly enough.

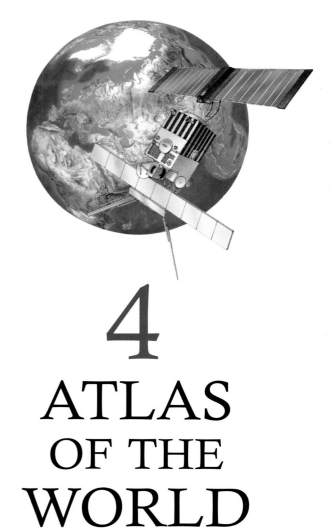

4
ATLAS
OF THE
WORLD

When the first maps were drawn, people knew very little about the planet on which they lived. The earliest maps of Africa to be drawn by Europeans showed vast expanses of blank territory in the center of the continent. Today, there are no blank pages in our atlases. Modern technology has made it possible to measure, survey and map the Earth in incredible detail. Maps describe the physical features of the land and oceans. They can also be used to show countries and their borders, historical events, population, climate, vegetation and natural resources.

Flags fluttering in the breeze – they are symbols of national identity.

MAPPING THE WORLD

Maps are images that show the surface of a planet such as Earth. The earliest maps were drawn to help travellers find their way. They showed coastlines and rivers, roads and towns. Maps are still used for the same purpose today – from maps of international flight paths to local street plans. However, as you have discovered from this atlas, all kinds of other information can be plotted on a map – from historical events to daily weather patterns.

ABOVE: Political maps show borders between countries, states or counties. Different regions may be shown in different colors.

LEFT: Physical maps represent features of the landscape. They show the height or "relief" of the land, mountain ranges, rivers and lakes, islands and shorelines.

Symbols and Scale

Maps include all kinds of symbols. A square may represent a capital city and a black line may represent a railway. The meaning of each symbol is normally explained in a key. The key also shows the scale to which the map is drawn. Large-scale maps can show every detail of a small area, even down to individual buidings. Small-scale maps make it possible to show very large regions on a single page.

ABOVE: Large-scale maps, such as those used by walkers, may show a mixture of physical and political features, roads and footpaths and important landmarks.

Round or flat?

The Earth is a sphere, so maps can only be completely accurate if they are drawn on a globe. Maps printed on a page have to show three-dimensional objects as if they were flat. Map-makers have worked out various ways of doing this and each of their systems is called a "projection." Projections such as the one shown below can be thought of as the skin from an orange (right) that has been peeled and spread out on a table (below). In order to make the "skin" completely flat, sections need to be cut out. On the map, these sections are removed from the oceans so that the shapes of the continents are not distorted too much.

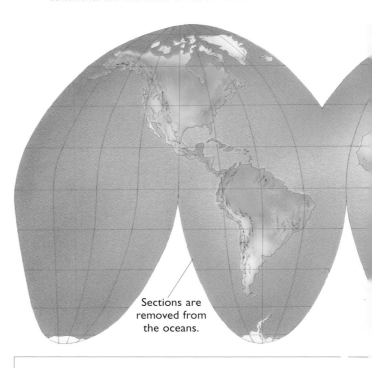

Sections are removed from the oceans.

Latitude lines

Longitude lines

Longitude and Latitude

Map-makers, or cartographers, have devised a grid of lines which criss-cross the globe (left). These allow us to pinpoint any spot on the surface of the Earth. Those which run from the North Pole to the South Pole are called lines of longitude. Those running around the world, parallel to the Equator, are called lines of latitude. Lines of longitude are measured in degrees east or west of the "prime meridian," which runs through Greenwich in London, while lines of latitude are given in degrees north or south of the Equator.

Cartographers at Work

Map-making is called cartography. The first maps were made on the spot, using a mixture of crude measurements and guesswork! Later, careful land surveys were carried out to compile more accurate maps that were printed from hand-drawn originals. Today, cartographic information can be provided by air and space surveys. All the data is fed into a computer which then generates the map (right).

MAP PROJECTIONS

In addition to the "orange peel" projections, there are three other types of projection that are commonly used. They differ in the way the grid lines on the globe are transferred on to a flat surface. In a **conical projection**, a paper cone is put over the globe. The grid lines appear on the paper as radiating lines. This has the effect of squashing the land masses nearest the poles and stretching those at the Equator. A **cylindrical projection** can be produced by wrapping a sheet of paper around the globe. The grid lines make squares and rectangles on the paper with the effect that the land masses near the Equator are squashed together and those near the poles are stretched. If the globe is balanced on a sheet of paper, the grid lines radiate outwards in an **azimuthal projection**. This projection is used, rather than the conical projection, for mapping small areas because it minimizes distortion.

Photograph A
The airplane flies at a constant height so that the scale of each photograph is the same.

Photograph B
The photographs overlap each other so that no areas are missed.

Photograph C
Information from the aerial photography is used to draw detailed maps.

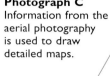
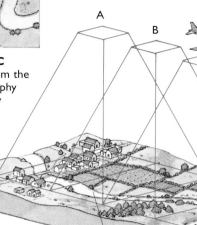

Aerial Photography

From the air, the view of the land below is very much like that of a map. The invention of flying in the 1900s made it possible to map the surface of the Earth more precisely than ever before. Powerful cameras on board remote-sensing aircraft take thousands of detailed, overlapping photographs. These images provide an accurate overview of huge areas, often revealing structures and patterns in the landscape that might not be seen in any other way.

ABOVE: A remote-sensing aircraft provides details for map-making. As the aircraft flies forward, an on-board camera takes a series of overlapping photographs – A, B and C.

Each overlapping section will appear in two consecutive photographs.

Solar panels generate electricity from sunlight to power the satellite.

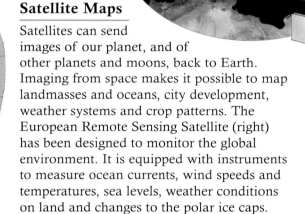

RIGHT: In this infrared satellite image of Europe and northern Africa, the red patches indicate cultivatable land and the grey areas represent a lack of vegetation, as in the desert regions of Africa.

Payload data handling system stores data or transmits it back to Earth.

Infrared sensors measure ocean temperatures and cloud cover.

Satellite Maps

Satellites can send images of our planet, and of other planets and moons, back to Earth. Imaging from space makes it possible to map landmasses and oceans, city development, weather systems and crop patterns. The European Remote Sensing Satellite (right) has been designed to monitor the global environment. It is equipped with instruments to measure ocean currents, wind speeds and temperatures, sea levels, weather conditions on land and changes to the polar ice caps.

Antennae collect images of the oceans, continents and polar ice caps.

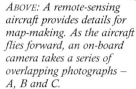
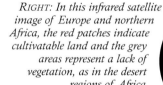
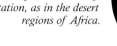

Minimal distortion to the shapes of the continents.

FANTASTIC FACTS

• The first photographic image of the Earth from space was taken by astronauts on the Apollo 8 mission circling the Moon on Christmas Day, December 25, 1968.

• The earliest known map dates back to 2250BC. It is etched on a clay tablet and shows the valley of the river Euphrates.

• In 1990 an atlas was sold for nearly $2 million in New York. The atlas was printed in 1486 and is based on maps devised in the 2nd century AD.

Conical projection of the northern hemisphere

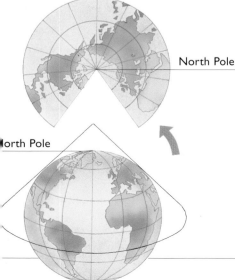

North Pole

North Pole

Cylindrical projection of the world

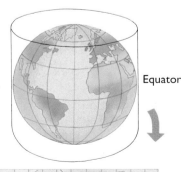

Equator

Equator

Azimuthal projection of part of the southern hemisphere

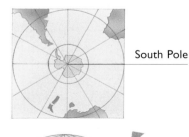

South Pole

South Pole

COUNTRIES OF THE WORLD

About 167 babies are born every minute and if the world's population continues to grow at current rates it will reach an estimated 6,158 million by the year 2000. However there is great inequality between the richest and the poorest nations in terms of education, healthcare and personal wealth.

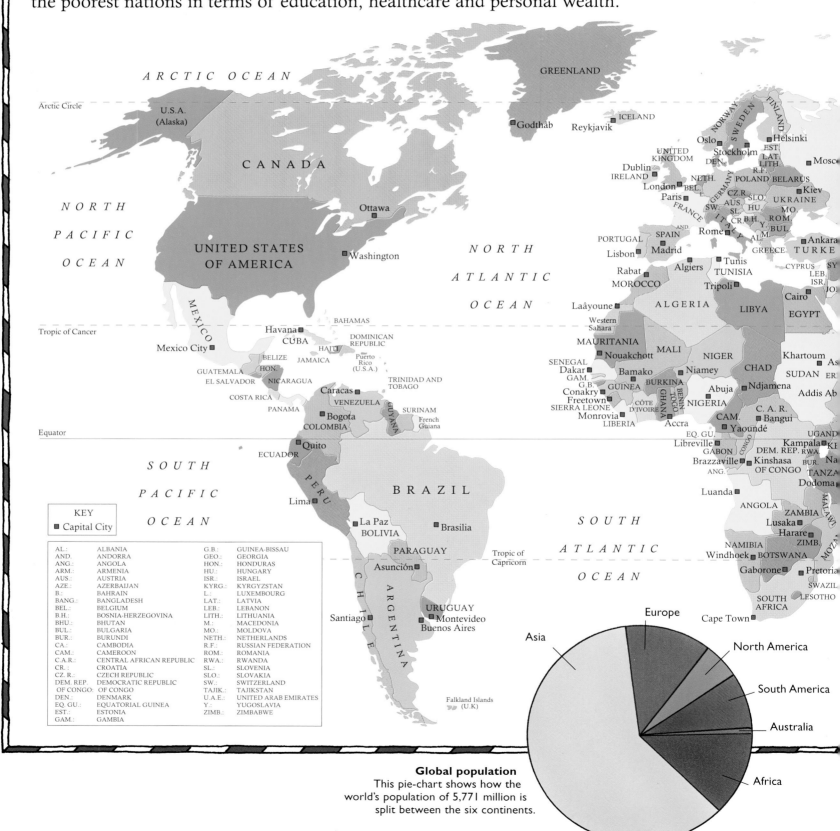

KEY
■ Capital City

AL.:	ALBANIA	G.B.:	GUINEA-BISSAU	
AND.:	ANDORRA	GEO.:	GEORGIA	
ANG.:	ANGOLA	HON.:	HONDURAS	
ARM.:	ARMENIA	HU.:	HUNGARY	
AUS.:	AUSTRIA	ISR.:	ISRAEL	
AZE.:	AZERBAIJAN	KYRG.:	KYRGYZSTAN	
B.:	BAHRAIN	L.:	LUXEMBOURG	
BANG.:	BANGLADESH	LAT.:	LATVIA	
BEL.:	BELGIUM	LEB.:	LEBANON	
B.H.:	BOSNIA-HERZEGOVINA	LITH.:	LITHUANIA	
BHU.:	BHUTAN	M.:	MACEDONIA	
BUL.:	BULGARIA	MO.:	MOLDOVA	
BUR.:	BURUNDI	NETH.:	NETHERLANDS	
CA.:	CAMBODIA	R.F.:	RUSSIAN FEDERATION	
CAM.:	CAMEROON	ROM.:	ROMANIA	
C.A.R.:	CENTRAL AFRICAN REPUBLIC	RWA.:	RWANDA	
CR.:	CROATIA	SL.:	SLOVENIA	
CZ. R.:	CZECH REPUBLIC	SLO.:	SLOVAKIA	
DEM. REP.	DEMOCRATIC REPUBLIC	SW.:	SWITZERLAND	
OF CONGO:	OF CONGO	TAJIK.:	TAJIKSTAN	
DEN.:	DENMARK	U.A.E.:	UNITED ARAB EMIRATES	
EQ. GU.:	EQUATORIAL GUINEA	Y.:	YUGOSLAVIA	
EST.:	ESTONIA	ZIMB.:	ZIMBABWE	
GAM.:	GAMBIA			

Global population
This pie-chart shows how the world's population of 5,771 million is split between the six continents.

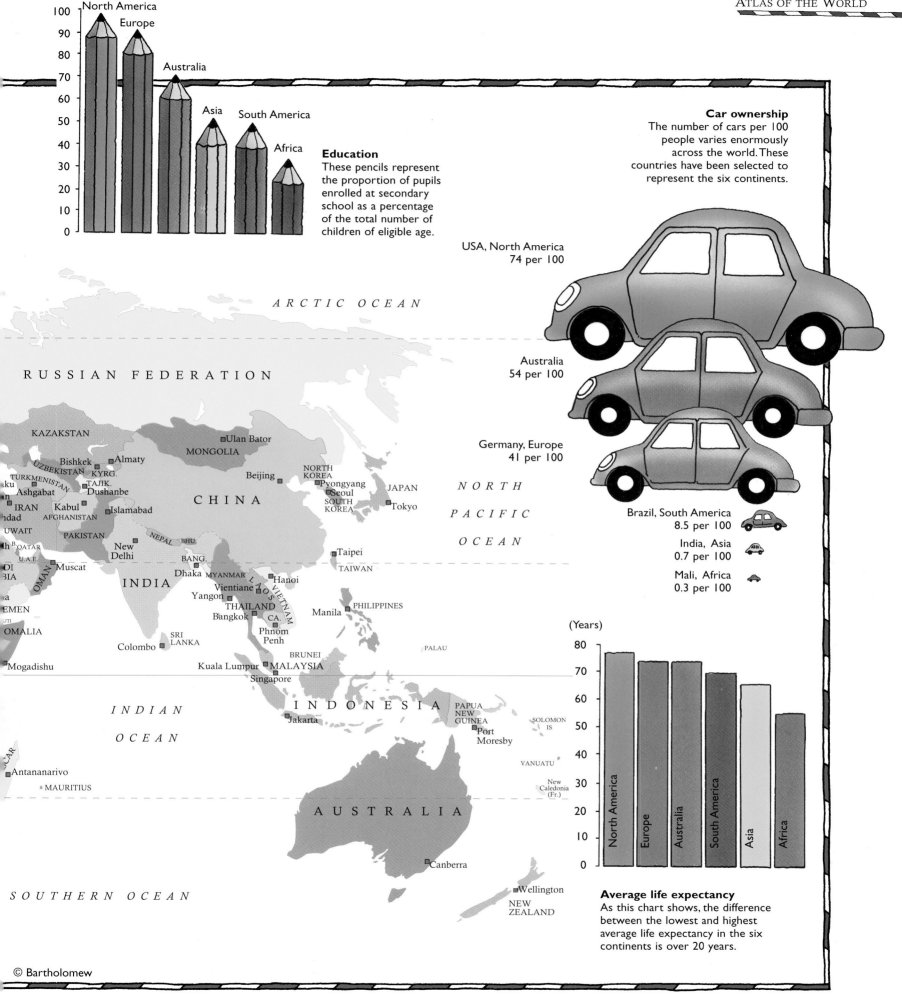

Education
These pencils represent the proportion of pupils enrolled at secondary school as a percentage of the total number of children of eligible age.

Car ownership
The number of cars per 100 people varies enormously across the world. These countries have been selected to represent the six continents.

USA, North America
74 per 100

Australia
54 per 100

Germany, Europe
41 per 100

Brazil, South America
8.5 per 100

India, Asia
0.7 per 100

Mali, Africa
0.3 per 100

Average life expectancy
As this chart shows, the difference between the lowest and highest average life expectancy in the six continents is over 20 years.

© Bartholomew

NORTH AMERICA, INCLUDING CENTRAL AMERICA AND THE CARIBBEAN ISLANDS

North America stretches from the ice-bound Arctic coasts of Greenland and Canada, to the tropical forests of southern Central America. The land includes high mountains and volcanoes, burning deserts, temperate woodlands and wide open prairies – natural grasslands which now produce much of the world's grain. There are also many sprawling cities.

NORTH AMERICA

Area: 9,100,000 sq mi

Biggest country: Canada

Biggest city: Mexico City

Highest point: Mount Denali or McKinley (20,323ft)

Lowest point: Death Valley (-282ft)

Longest river: Mississippi-Missouri (3,740mi)

Biggest lake: Superior (27,750 sq mi)

NORTHERN NORTH AMERICA

BERMUDA
[United Kingdom]
Capital: Hamilton
Population: 75,000
Area: 21 sq mi

CANADA
Capital: Ottawa
Population: 28,753,000
Area: 3,849,674 sq mi

GREENLAND
[Denmark]
Capital: Nuuk (Godthab)
Population: 57,000
Area: 840,004 sq mi

MEXICO
Capital: Mexico City
Population: 91,261,000
Area: 758,452 sq mi

ST PIERRE & MIQUELON
[France]
Capital: St Pierre
Population: 6,500
Area: 93 sq mi

UNITED STATES OF AMERICA
Capital: Washington DC
Population:255,020,000
Area: 3,717,796 sq mi

CENTRAL AMERICA

BELIZE
Capital: Belmopan
Population: 189,400
Area: 8,867 sq mi

COSTA RICA
Capital: San José
Population: 3,199,000
Area: 19,714 sq mi

EL SALVADOR
Capital: San Salvador
Population: 5,517,000
Area: 8,124 sq mi

GUATEMALA
Capital: Guatemala City
Population: 9,745,000
Area: 42,042 sq mi

HONDURAS
Capital: Tegucigalpa
Population: 28,753,000
Area: 43,433 sq mi

NICARAGUA
Capital: Managua
Population: 4,265,000
Area: 49,998 sq mi

PANAMA
Capital: Panama City
Population: 2,535,000
Area: 29,157 sq mi

CARIBBEAN ISLANDS

ANGUILLA
[United Kingdom]
Capital: The Valley
Population: 8,960
Area: 36 sq mi

ANTIGUA & BARBUDA
Capital: St John's
Population: 67,000
Area: 171 sq mi

ARUBA
[Netherlands]
Capital: Oranjestad
Population: 69,000
Area: 75 sq mi

THE BAHAMAS
Capital: Nassau
Population: 269,000
Area: 5,382 sq mi

BARBADOS
Capital: Bridgetown
Population: 260,000
Area: 166 sq mi

CAYMAN ISLANDS
[United Kingdom]
Capital: George Town
Population: 29,000
Area: 101 sq mi

CUBA
Capital: Havana
Population: 11,000,000
Area: 44,218 sq mi

DOMINICA
Capital: Roseau
Population: 88,000
Area: 289 sq mi

DOMINICAN REPUBLIC
Capital: Santo Domingo
Population: 7,608,000
Area: 18,700 sq mi

GRENADA
Capital: St George's
Population: 95,000
Area: 133 sq mi

GUADELOUPE
[France]
Capital: Basse-Terre
Population: 400,000
Area: 687 sq mi

HAITI
Capital: Port-au-Prince
Population: 6,903,000
Area: 10,714 sq mi

JAMAICA
Capital: Kingston
Population: 2,523,000
Area: 4,244 sq mi

MARTINIQUE
[France]
Capital: Fort-de-France
Population: 373,000
Area: 425 sq mi

MONTSERRAT
[United Kingdom]
Capital: Plymouth
Population: 13,000
Area: 39 sq mi

NETHERLANDS ANTILLES
[Netherlands]
Capital: Willemstad
Population: 191,000
Area: 283 sq mi

PUERTO RICO
[USA]
Capital: San Juan
Population: 3,620,000
Area: 3,515 sq mi

ST KITTS-NEVIS
Capital: Basseterre
Population: 44,000
Area: 104 sq mi

ST LUCIA
Capital: Castries
Population: 139,000
Area: 238 sq mi

Dominica

Antigua and Barbuda

St Kitts-Nevis

Dominican Republic

Haiti

Jamaica

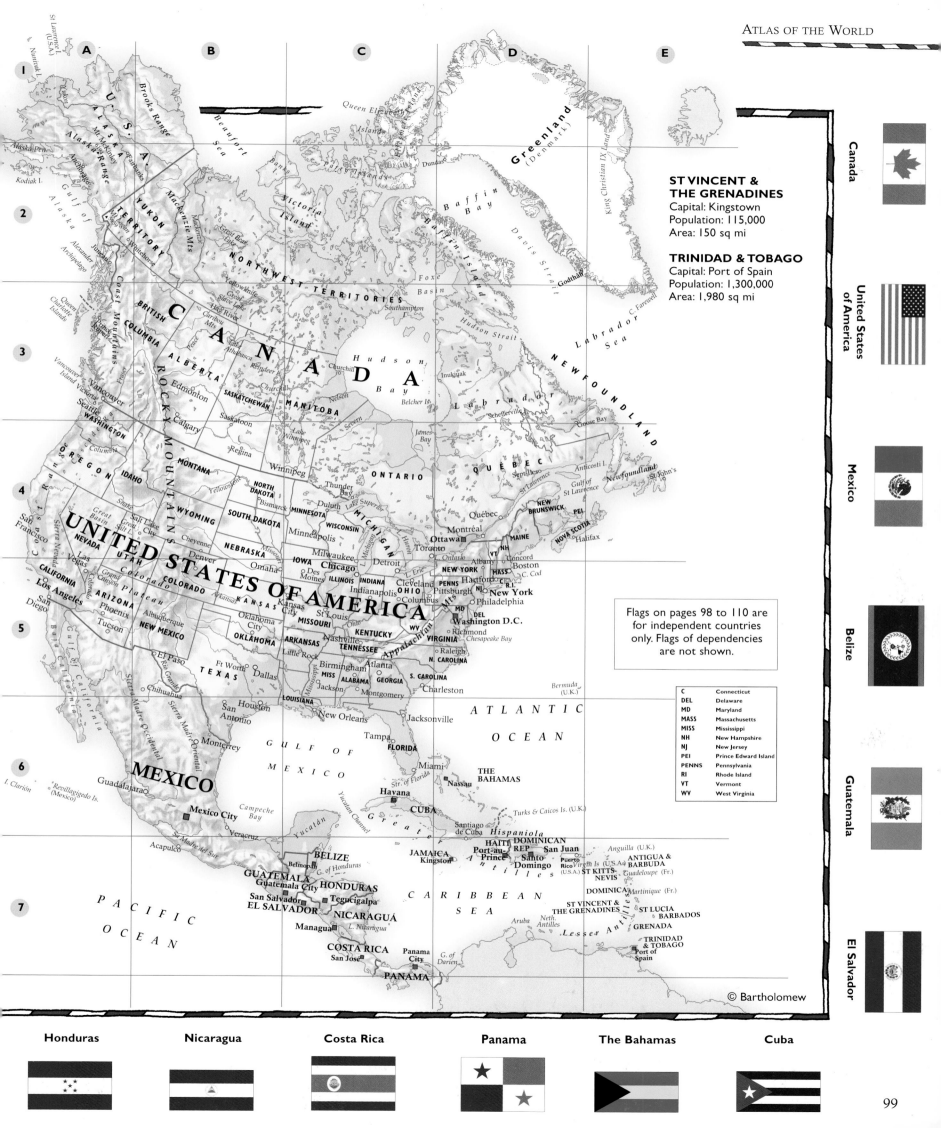

ST VINCENT & THE GRENADINES
Capital: Kingstown
Population: 115,000
Area: 150 sq mi

TRINIDAD & TOBAGO
Capital: Port of Spain
Population: 1,300,000
Area: 1,980 sq mi

Flags on pages 98 to 110 are for independent countries only. Flags of dependencies are not shown.

C	Connecticut
DEL	Delaware
MD	Maryland
MASS	Massachusetts
MISS	Mississippi
NH	New Hampshire
NJ	New Jersey
PEI	Prince Edward Island
PENNS	Pennsylvania
RI	Rhode Island
VT	Vermont
WV	West Virginia

© Bartholomew

Canada

United States of America

Mexico

Belize

Guatemala

El Salvador

Honduras

Nicaragua

Costa Rica

Panama

The Bahamas

Cuba

SOUTH AMERICA

South America is bordered to the north by the Caribbean Sea, to the east by the Atlantic Ocean and to the west by the Pacific Ocean. It is joined to the rest of the Americas by a narrow strip of land called the Isthmus of Panama. The high mountain chain of the Andes runs like a backbone from north to south. The continent takes in the world's largest rainforests, deserts, grasslands and bleak plateaus.

Galapagos Island (Ecuador)

GUYANA
Capital: Georgetown
Population: 816,000
Area: 83,000 sq mi

PARAGUAY
Capital: Asunción
Population: 4,643,000
Area: 157,048 sq mi

PERU
Capital: Lima
Population: 22,454,000
Area: 494,200 sq mi

SURINAM
Capital: Paramaribo
Population: 446,000
Area: 63,037 sq mi

URUGUAY
Capital: Montevideo
Population: 3,200,000
Area: 68,037 sq mi

VENEZUELA
Capital: Caracas
Population: 20,712,000
Area: 352,144 sq mi

LEFT: Sugar Loaf Mountain stands at the entrance to the harbour in Rio de Janeiro, Brazil's second-largest city.

ARGENTINA
Capital: Buenos Aires
Population: 33,778,000
Area: 1,073,518 sq mi

BOLIVIA
Capital: La Paz
Population: 8,010,000
Area: 424,164 sq mi

BRAZIL
Capital: Brasília
Population: 159,100,000
Area: 3,300,171 sq mi

CHILE
Capital: Santiago
Population: 13,813,000
Area: 292,135 sq mi

COLOMBIA
Capital: Bogotá
Population: 34,900,800
Area: 440,831 sq mi

ECUADOR
Capital: Quito
Population: 10,980,000
Area: 105,037 sq mi

FALKLAND ISLANDS
[United Kingdom]
Capital: Stanley
Population: 2,100
Area: 4,700 sq mi

FRENCH GUIANA
[France]
Capital: Cayenne
Population: 115,000
Area: 35,135 sq mi

RIGHT: The great Amazon River snakes across Peru and northern Brazil. It passes through the world's largest area of dense rainforest where communities of indigenous peoples still live.

Ecuador

Colombia

Venezuela

Guyana

Surinam

Brazil

A   B   C   D   E

I

1

Barranquilla
Cartagena
G. of Darien
Maracaibo
Valencia
Caracas
Orinoco Delta
L. Maracaibo
Orinoco
Georgetown
Paramaribo
Cayenne

2

Medellín
VENEZUELA
GUYANA
SURINAM
French Guiana

ATLANTIC

Magdalena
Llanos
Bogotá
COLOMBIA
Cali

OCEAN

Cotopaxi 5896
Quito
ECUADOR
Chimborazo 6310
Guayaquil

Negro
Amazon Delta
I. de Marajó
Belém
Fortaleza

3

Iquitos
Amazon
Jurúa
Purús
Manaus
Amazon
Tapajós

S e l v a s

Trujillo
Huascaran 6768

A N D E S

B R A Z I L

Porto Velho
Madeira
Araguaia
Tocantins
São Francisco
Recife

4

P E R U

Lima
Cusco

Lake Titicaca

Arequipa

Planalto do Mato Grosso

Planalto Brasil

Brasília

Salvador

La Paz
Santa Cruz
BOLIVIA

Belo Horizonte

5

PACIFIC

Antofagasta

Atacama Desert

Gran Chaco

PARAGUAY

Asunción
Formosa

Paraná

São Paulo
Rio de Janeiro

Curitiba

OCEAN

Islas de los Desventurados
(Chile)

Uruguay

6

Juan Fernandez Islands
(Chile)

Aconcagua 6960

Catamarca

Córdoba

P a m p a s

Valparaíso
Mendoza
Santiago

A R G E N T I N A

C H I L E

A N D E S

URUGUAY

Buenos Aires
Montevideo

Río de la Plata

Concepcion
Colorado
Bahía Blanca

7

Puerto Montt

P A T A G O N I A

Comodoro Rivadavia

SOUTH AMERICA

Total area: 6,880,000 sq mi

Biggest country: Brazil

Biggest city: São Paulo

Highest point: Mount Aconcagua (22,832ft)

Lowest point: Peninsula Valdés (-131ft)

Longest river: Amazon (4,049ft)

Biggest lake: Titicaca (2,880 sq mi)

© Bartholomew

8

Punta Atenos
Strait of Magellan
Falkland Islands
(U.K.)
South Georgia
(U.K.)
Tierra del Fuego
Cape Horn

Peru

Bolivia

Paraguay

Uruguay

Argentina

Chile

101

| Denmark | Norway | Sweden | Finland | Iceland | Republic of Ireland | United Kingdom |

EUROPE

Europe is part of the same land mass as Asia and its eastern borders lies along the Ural Mountains. To the west is the Atlantic Ocean, and to the south are the Mediterranean, Black and Caspian Seas. The northern coasts border the frozen Arctic, but the west has a mild, moist climate. Southern lands have hot, dry summers.

SCANDINAVIA

DENMARK
Capital: Copenhagen
Population: 5,189,000
Area: 16,639 sq mi

NORWAY
Capital: Oslo
Population: 4,312,000
Area: 148,896 sq mi

SWEDEN
Capital: Stockholm
Population: 8,721,000
Area: 173,732 sq mi

FINLAND
Capital: Helsinki
Population: 5,069,000
Area: 130,559 sq mi

WESTERN EUROPE

ANDORRA
Capital: Andorra la Vella
Population: 62,000
Area: 181 sq mi

AUSTRIA
Capital: Vienna
Population: 7,988,000
Area: 32,378 sq mi

AZORES
[Portugal]
Capital: Ponta Delgada
Population:238,000
Area: 868 sq mi

BELGIUM
Capital: Brussels
Population: 10,050,000
Area: 11,787 sq mi

CHANNEL ISLANDS
[United Kingdom]
Capitals: St Helier,
St Peter Port
Population:144,000
Area: 62 sq mi

FAEROE ISLANDS
[Denmark]
Capital: Torshavn
Population: 47,000
Area: 540 sq mi

FRANCE
Capital: Paris
Population: 57,800,000
Area: 210,026 sq mi

GERMANY
Capital: Berlin
Population: 81,187,000
Area: 137,827 sq mi

GIBRALTAR
[United Kingdom]
Capital: Gibraltar
Population: 31,000
Area: 2 sq mi

ICELAND
Capital: Reykjavik
Population: 270,000
Area: 39,800 sq mi

ITALY
Capital: Rome
Population: 58,100,000
Area: 116,341 sq mi

LIECHTENSTEIN
Capital: Vaduz
Population: 30,000
Area: 62 sq mi

LUXEMBOURG
Capital: Luxembourg City
Population: 395,000
Area: 998 sq mi

MADEIRA
[Portugal]
Capital: Funchal
Population: 254,000
Area: 307 sq mi

MALTA
Capital: Valletta
Population: 365,000
Area: 122 sq mi

MONACO
Capital: Monaco
Population: 28,000
Area: .75 sq mi

NETHERLANDS
Capital: Amsterdam
Population: 15,287,000
Area: 16,033 sq mi

PORTUGAL
Capital: Lisbon
Population: 10,450,000
Area: 34,485 sq mi

REPUBLIC OF IRELAND
Capital: Dublin
Population: 3,600,000
Area: 27,133 sq mi

SAN MARINO
Capital: San Marino
Population: 24,000
Area: 23 sq mi

SPAIN
Capital: Madrid
Population: 39,200,000
Area: 195,364 sq mi

SWITZERLAND
Capital: Bern
Population: 6,938,000
Area: 15,940 sq mi

UNITED KINGDOM
Capital: London
Population: 58,000,000
Area: 94,251 sq mi

VATICAN CITY
Capital: Vatican City
Population: 1,000
Area: 110 acres

CENTRAL EUROPE

ALBANIA
Capital: Tirana
Population: 3,400,000
Area: 11,100 sq mi

BOSNIA-HERZEGOVINA
Capital: Sarajevo
Population: 4,400,000
Area: 30,677 sq mi

BULGARIA
Capital: Sofia
Population: 9,020,000
Area: 42,855 sq mi

CROATIA
Capital: Zagreb
Population: 4,850,000
Area: 21,819 sq mi

CZECH REPUBLIC
Capital: Prague
Population: 10,330,000
Area: 30,450 sq mi

CYPRUS
Capital: Nicosia
Population: 725,000
Area: 3,572 sq mi

ESTONIA
Capital: Tallinn
Population: 1,620,000
Area: 17,462 sq mi

GREECE
Capital: Athens
Population: 10,350,000
Area: 50,949 sq mi

HUNGARY
Capital: Budapest
Population: 10,310,000
Area: 35,919 sq mi

LATVIA
Capital: Riga
Population: 2,610,000
Area: 24,600 sq mi

LITHUANIA
Capital: Vilnius
Population: 3,742,000
Area: 25,200 sq mi

MACEDONIA
[Former Yugoslav Republic]
Capital: Skopje
Population: 2,173,000
Area: 9,928 sq mi

POLAND
Capital: Warsaw
Population: 38,459,000
Area: 120,728 sq mi

ROMANIA
Capital: Bucharest
Population: 23,200,000
Area: 91,700 sq mi

SLOVAKIA
Capital: Bratislava
Population: 5,320,000
Area: 18,933 sq mi

SLOVENIA
Capital: Ljubljana
Population: 2,000,000
Area: 7,820 sq mi

TURKEY
[partly in Europe]
Capital: Ankara
Population: 58,870,000
Area: 300,948 sq mi

YUGOSLAVIA
[Serbia-Montenegro]
Capital: Belgrade
Population: 10,485,000
Area: 39,449 sq mi

EASTERN EUROPE

BELARUS
Capital: Minsk
Population: 10,400,000
Area: 80,153 sq mi

MOLDOVA
Capital: Chisinau
Population: 4,500,000
Area: 13,000 sq mi

RUSSIAN FEDERATION
[also in Asia]
Capital: Moscow
Population: 150,000,000
Area: 6,592,770 sq mi

UKRAINE
Capital: Kiev
Population: 52,194,000
Area: 233,100 sq mi

Moldova
Ukraine
Belarus
Russian Federation
Cyprus
Romania
Bulgaria
Greece
Albania

| Turkey | Macedonia | Yugoslavia | Bosnia-Herzegovina | Croatia | Slovenia | Hungary |

102

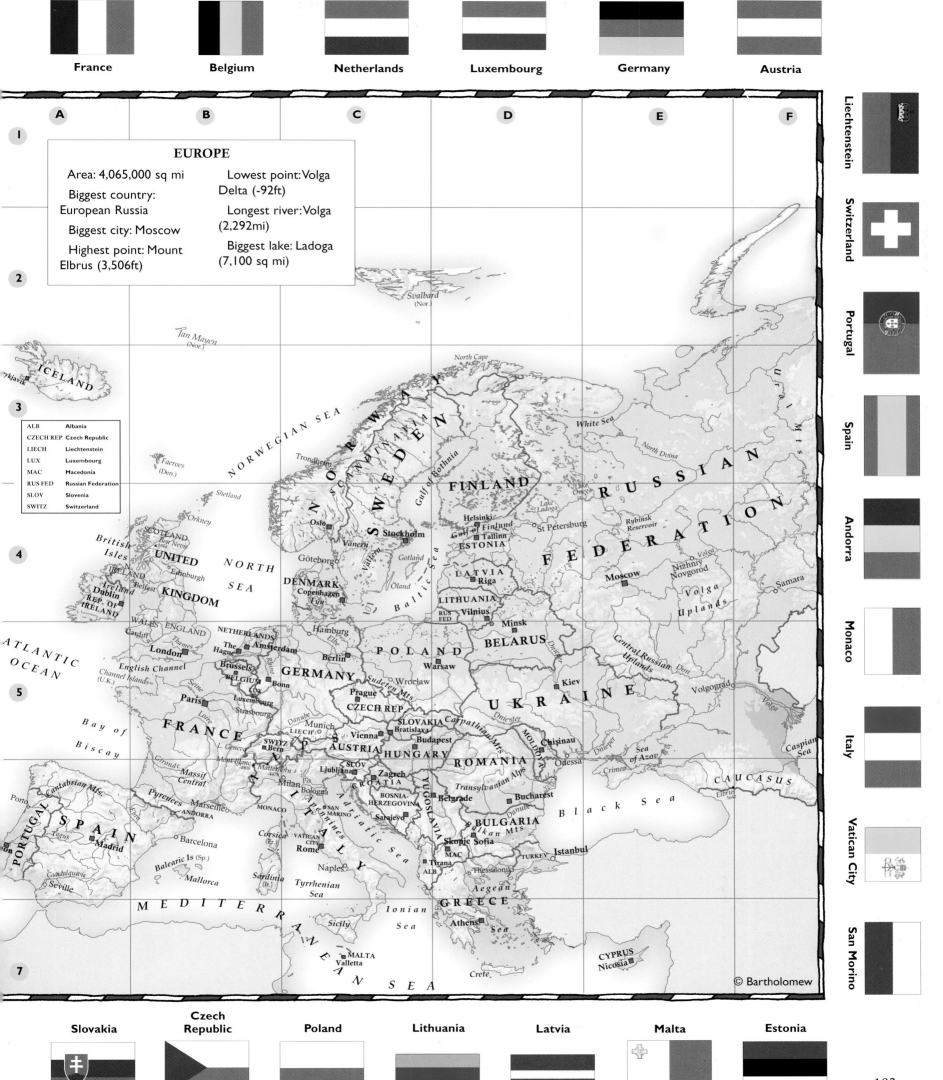

France

Belgium

Netherlands

Luxembourg

Germany

Austria

Liechtenstein

Switzerland

Portugal

Spain

Andorra

Monaco

Italy

Vatican City

San Morino

EUROPE

Area: 4,065,000 sq mi

Biggest country: European Russia

Biggest city: Moscow

Highest point: Mount Elbrus (3,506ft)

Lowest point: Volga Delta (-92ft)

Longest river: Volga (2,292mi)

Biggest lake: Ladoga (7,100 sq mi)

ALB	Albania
CZECH REP	Czech Republic
LIECH	Liechtenstein
LUX	Luxembourg
MAC	Macedonia
RUS FED	Russian Federation
SLOV	Slovenia
SWITZ	Switzerland

© Bartholomew

Slovakia

Czech Republic

Poland

Lithuania

Latvia

Malta

Estonia

103

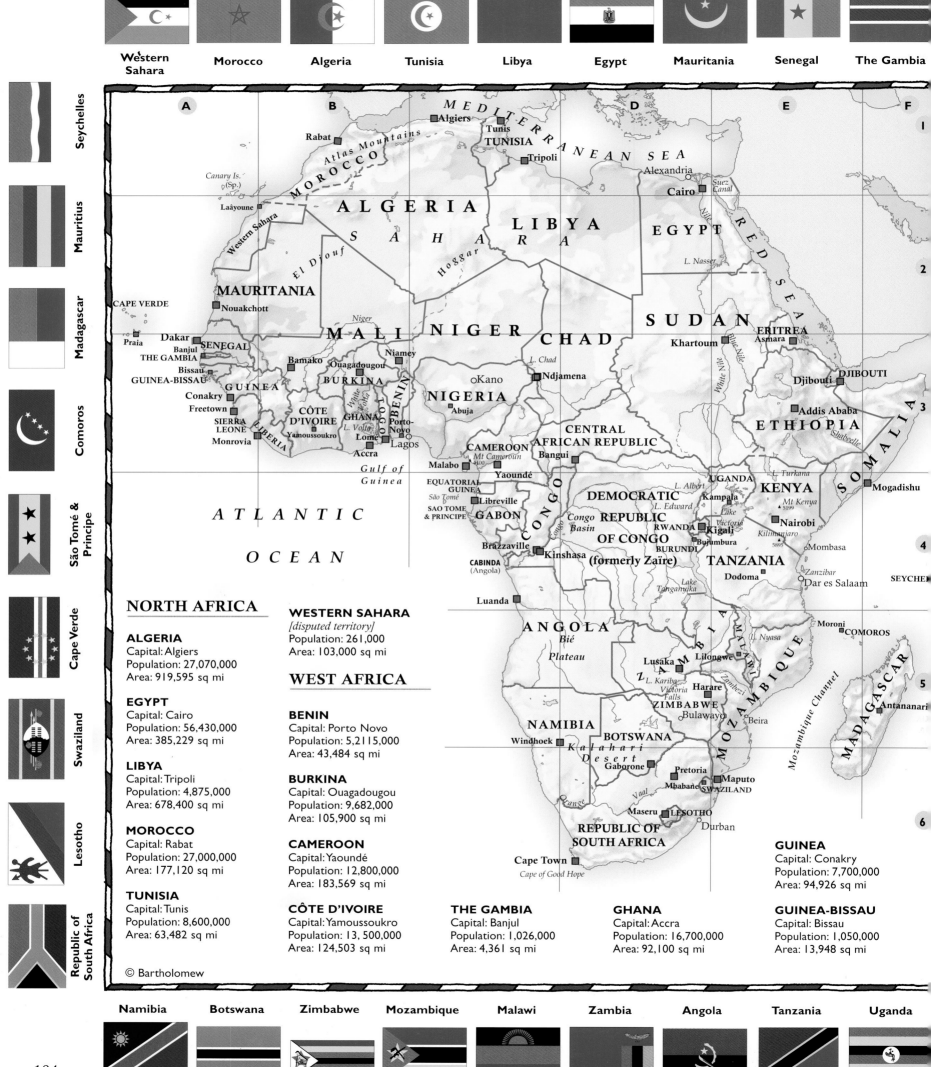

Western Sahara · **Morocco** · **Algeria** · **Tunisia** · **Libya** · **Egypt** · **Mauritania** · **Senegal** · **The Gambia**

Seychelles · Mauritius · Madagascar · Comoros · São Tomé & Príncipe · Cape Verde · Swaziland · Lesotho · Republic of South Africa

NORTH AFRICA

ALGERIA
Capital: Algiers
Population: 27,070,000
Area: 919,595 sq mi

EGYPT
Capital: Cairo
Population: 56,430,000
Area: 385,229 sq mi

LIBYA
Capital: Tripoli
Population: 4,875,000
Area: 678,400 sq mi

MOROCCO
Capital: Rabat
Population: 27,000,000
Area: 177,120 sq mi

TUNISIA
Capital: Tunis
Population: 8,600,000
Area: 63,482 sq mi

WESTERN SAHARA
[disputed territory]
Population: 261,000
Area: 103,000 sq mi

WEST AFRICA

BENIN
Capital: Porto Novo
Population: 5,2115,000
Area: 43,484 sq mi

BURKINA
Capital: Ouagadougou
Population: 9,682,000
Area: 105,900 sq mi

CAMEROON
Capital: Yaoundé
Population: 12,800,000
Area: 183,569 sq mi

CÔTE D'IVOIRE
Capital: Yamoussoukro
Population: 13, 500,000
Area: 124,503 sq mi

THE GAMBIA
Capital: Banjul
Population: 1,026,000
Area: 4,361 sq mi

GHANA
Capital: Accra
Population: 16,700,000
Area: 92,100 sq mi

GUINEA
Capital: Conakry
Population: 7,700,000
Area: 94,926 sq mi

GUINEA-BISSAU
Capital: Bissau
Population: 1,050,000
Area: 13,948 sq mi

© Bartholomew

104

Namibia · **Botswana** · **Zimbabwe** · **Mozambique** · **Malawi** · **Zambia** · **Angola** · **Tanzania** · **Uganda**

AFRICA

The continent of Africa lies across the Equator, between the Atlantic and Indian Oceans and the Mediterranean Sea to the north. It includes the world's largest desert, the Sahara, equatorial rainforests and large areas of rolling savannah, the home of some of the last great herds of wild animals. During the 19thcentury much of Africa was brought under colonial rule but today it is a continent of independent nation states.

AFRICA

Area: 11,710,000 sq mi

Biggest country: Sudan

Biggest city: Cairo

Highest point: Mount Kilimanjaro (19,342ft)

Lowest point: Lac' Assal (-512ft)

Longest river: Nile (4,160mi)

Biggest lake: Victoria (26,830 sq mi)

LIBERIA
Capital: Monrovia
Population: 2,700,000
Area: 38,250 sq mi

MALI
Capital: Bamako
Population: 10,137,000
Area: 478,841 sq mi

MAURITANIA
Capital: Nouakchott
Population: 2,206,000
Area: 398,000 sq mi

NIGER
Capital: Niamey
Population: 8,500,000
Area: 489,200 sq mi

NIGERIA
Capital: Abuja
Population: 119,328,000
Area: 356,669 sq mi

SENEGAL
Capital: Dakar
Population: 7,970,000
Area: 75,955 sq mi

SIERRA LEONE
Capital: Freetown
Population: 4,494,000
Area: 27,699 sq mi

TOGO
Capital: Lomé
Population: 4,100,000
Area: 21,925 sq mi

CENTRAL AFRICA

BURUNDI
Capital: Bujumbura
Population: 5,958,000
Area: 10,747 sq mi

CENTRAL AFRICAN REPUBLIC
Capital: Bangui
Population: 3,258,000
Area: 240,324 sq mi

CHAD
Capital: Ndjamena
Population: 6,290,000
Area: 495,800 sq mi

CONGO
Capital: Brazzaville
Population: 2,700,000
Area: 132,000 sq mi

DEMOCRATIC REPUBLIC OF CONGO
Capital: Kinshasa
Population: 41,166,000
Area: 905,365 sq mi

EQUATORIAL GUINEA
Capital: Malabo
Population: 390,000
Area: 10,831 sq mi

GABON
Capital: Libreville
Population: 1,012,000
Area: 103,347 sq mi

RWANDA
Capital: Kigali
Population: 7,700,000
Area: 10,169 sq mi

EAST AFRICA

DJIBOUTI
Capital: Djibouti
Population: 481,000
Area: 8,958 sq mi

ERITREA
Capital: Asmara
Population: 3,500,000
Area: 46,774 sq mi

ETHIOPIA
Capital: Addis Ababa
Population: 56,900,000
Area: 437,600 sq mi

KENYA
Capital: Nairobi
Population: 28,113,000
Area: 224,961 sq mi

SOMALIA
Capital: Mogadishu
Population: 9,517,000
Area: 246,200 sq mi

SUDAN
Capital: Khartoum
Population: 30,830,000
Area: 967,500 sq mi

TANZANIA
Capital: Dodoma
Population: 28,783,000
Area: 364,900 sq mi

UGANDA
Capital: Kampala
Population: 19,246,000
Area: 93,104 sq mi

SOUTHERN AFRICA

ANGOLA
Capital: Luanda
Population: 10,770,000
Area: 481,350 sq mi

BOTSWANA
Capital: Gaborone
Population: 1,400,000
Area: 224,607 sq mi

LESOTHO
Capital: Maseru
Population: 1,900,000
Area: 11,720 sq mi

MALAWI
Capital: Lilongwe
Population: 9,700,000
Area: 45,747 sq mi

MOZAMBIQUE
Capital: Maputo
Population: 16,600,000
Area: 308,642 sq mi

NAMIBIA
Capital: Windhoek
Population: 1,550,000
Area: 318,252 sq mi

REPUBLIC OF SOUTH AFRICA
Capitals: Capetown, Pretoria
Population: 40,774,000
Area: 470,693 sq mi

SWAZILAND
Capital: Mbabane
Population: 835,000
Area: 6,704 sq mi

ZAMBIA
Capital: Lusaka
Population: 9,000,000
Area: 290,586 sq mi

ZIMBABWE
Capital: Harare
Population: 10,898,000
Area: 150,873 sq mi

ISLANDS

CAPE VERDE
Capital: Praia
Population: 395,000
Area: 1,557 sq mi

COMOROS
Capital: Moroni
Population: 607,000
Area: 719 sq mi

MADAGASCAR
Capital: Antananarivo
Population: 13,259,000
Area: 226,658 sq mi

MAURITIUS
Capital: Port Louis
Population: 1,100,000
Area: 788 sq mi

REUNION *[France]*
Capital: St Denis
Population: 624,000
Area: 970 sq mi

SAO TOME & PRINCIPE
Capital: São Tomé & Principe
Population: 130,000
Area: 386 sq mi

SEYCHELLES
Capital: Victoria
Population: 80,000
Area: 175 sq mi

 Kenya **Somalia** **Ethiopia** **Djibouti** **Eritrea** **Sudan** **Burundi** **Rwanda** **Democratic Repub. of Congo**

105

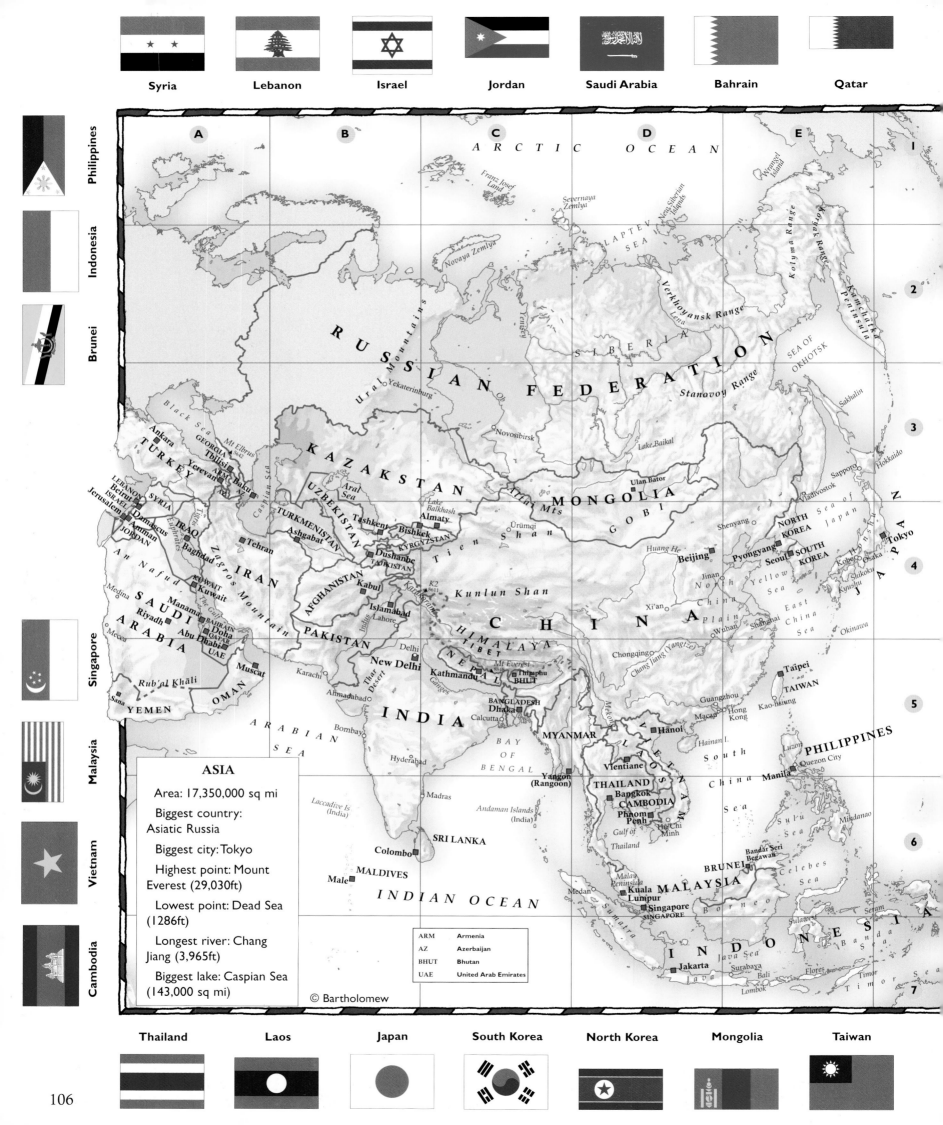

Syria Lebanon Israel Jordan Saudi Arabia Bahrain Qatar

Philippines
Indonesia
Brunei
Singapore
Malaysia
Vietnam
Cambodia

A **B** **C** **D** **E**

A R C T I C   O C E A N

Franz Josef Land
Severnaya Zemlya
Novaya Zemlya

LAPTEV SEA
New Siberian Islands
Wrangel Island
Kolyma Range
Chukchi Range
Kamchatka Peninsula

R U S S I A N   F E D E R A T I O N

Ural Mountains
Yekaterinburg
Ob
Yenisey
Lena
Verkhoyansk Range
S I B E R I A
Stanovoy Range
SEA OF OKHOTSK
Sakhalin

Black Sea
Ankara
T U R K E Y
GEORGIA
Mt Elbrus 5642
Tbilisi
Yerevan
ARM. Baku
AZ.
Caspian Sea
Aral Sea
K A Z A K S T A N
Novosibirsk
Lake Balkhash
Altai Mts
Lake Baikal
M O N G O L I A
Ulan Bator
G O B I
Hokkaido
Sapporo

LEBANON
Beirut
ISRAEL
Jerusalem
SYRIA
Damascus
Amman
JORDAN
IRAQ
Baghdad
Tigris
Euphrates
UZBEKISTAN
Tashkent
Lake
Almaty
Bishkek
KYRGYZSTAN
Dushanbe
TAJIKISTAN
Tien Shan
Ürümqi
Huang He
Beijing
Shenyang
NORTH KOREA
Pyongyang
Seoul SOUTH KOREA
Sea of Japan
Vladivostok
Tokyo
Honshu
J A P A N

Medina
Mecca
SAUDI ARABIA
Riyadh
KUWAIT
Kuwait
The Gulf
BAHRAIN
Manama
Doha
QATAR
Abu Dhabi
UAE
Muscat
An Nafud
Zagros Mountains
I R A N
Tehran
Ashgabat
TURKMENISTAN
AFGHANISTAN
Kabul
Islamabad
Lahore
Indus
K2 8611
Karakoram
Kunlun Shan
C H I N A
Xi'an
Jinan
Yellow Sea
Kobe Osaka
Shikoku
Kyushu
Okinawa
East China Sea
North China Plain
Wuhan
Shanghai

Rub'al Khāli
YEMEN
Sana
O M A N
PAKISTAN
Karachi
Ahmadabad
Thar Desert
New Delhi
Delhi
Ganges
Kathmandu
NEPAL
H I M A L A Y A
TIBET
Mt Everest 8848
Thimphu
BHUT.
BANGLADESH
Dhaka
Calcutta
Chongqing
Chang Jiang (Yangtze)
Guangzhou
Macau Hong Kong
Kao-hsiung
Taipei
TAIWAN

A R A B I A N   S E A
I N D I A
Bombay
Hyderabad
Madras
BAY OF BENGAL
MYANMAR
Yangon (Rangoon)
THAILAND
Bangkok
Mekong
Hanoi
Vientiane
LAOS
V I E T N A M
Hainan I.
South China Sea
Manila
Quezon City
Luzon
PHILIPPINES

ASIA

Area: 17,350,000 sq mi

Biggest country: Asiatic Russia

Biggest city: Tokyo

Highest point: Mount Everest (29,030ft)

Lowest point: Dead Sea (1286ft)

Longest river: Chang Jiang (3,965ft)

Biggest lake: Caspian Sea (143,000 sq mi)

Laccadive Is (India)
Andaman Islands (India)
Colombo
SRI LANKA
Male
MALDIVES
Gulf of Thailand
CAMBODIA
Phnom Penh
Ho Chi Minh
Sulu Sea
Mindanao
Celebes Sea
BRUNEI
Bandar Seri Begawan

I N D I A N   O C E A N
Medan
Malay Peninsula
Kuala Lumpur
Singapore
SINGAPORE
Sumatra
Borneo
MALAYSIA
I N D O N E S I A
Sulawesi
Seram
Banda Sea

Jakarta
Java Sea
Surabaya
Bali
Java
Lombok
Flores
Timor Sea
Timor

ARM	Armenia
AZ	Azerbaijan
BHUT	Bhutan
UAE	United Arab Emirates

© Bartholomew

1 **2** **3** **4** **5** **6** **7**

Thailand Laos Japan South Korea North Korea Mongolia Taiwan

106

 **United Arab Emirates**  **Yemen**  **Oman**   **Kuwait**   **Iraq** Iran  **Georgia**

ASIA

Asia is the largest continent of all, stretching from the Mediterranean Sea to the Pacific Ocean. It includes some of the most crowded lands on Earth as well as vast tracts of empty wilderness.

NEAR AND MIDDLE EAST

BAHRAIN
Capital: Manamah
Population: 539,000
Area: 273 sq mi

IRAN
Capital: Tehran
Population: 63,180,000
Area: 636,300 sq mi

IRAQ
Capital: Baghdad
Population: 19,918,000
Area: 169,235 sq mi

ISRAEL
[including autonomous Palestinian territories]
Capital: Jerusalem
Population: 5,300,000
Area: 8,473 sq mi

JORDAN
Capital: Amman
Population: 4,440,000
Area: 34,578 sq mi

KUWAIT
Capital: Kuwait
Population: 1,600,000
Area: 6,880 sq mi

LEBANON
Capital: Beirut
Population: 2,900,000
Area: 4,036 sq mi

OMAN
Capital: Muscat
Population: 1,697,000
Area: 119,500 sq mi

QATAR
Capital: Doha
Population: 559,000
Area: 4,412 sq mi

SAUDI ARABIA
Capital: Riyadh
Population: 17,500,000
Area: 864,900 sq mi

SYRIA
Capital: Damascus
Population: 13,400,000
Area: 71,498 sq mi

TURKEY
See Europe

UNITED ARAB EMIRATES
Capital: Abu Dhabi
Population: 2,100,000
Area: 32,300 sq mi

YEMEN
Capital: Sana
Population: 13,000,000
Area: 203,850 sq mi

CENTRAL ASIA

AFGHANISTAN
Capital: Kabul
Population: 20,547,000
Area: 251,825 sq mi

ARMENIA
Capital: Yerevan
Population: 3,677,000
Area: 11,500 sq mi

AZERBAIJAN
Capital: Baku
Population: 7,392,000
Area: 33,400 sq mi

GEORGIA
[also in Asia]
Capital: Tbilisi
Population: 5,471,000
Area: 26,900 sq mi

KAZAKSTAN
Capital: Almaty
Population: 17,200,000
Area: 1,049,200 sq mi

KYRGYZSTAN
Capital: Bishkek
Population: 4,600,000
Area: 76,640 sq mi

RUSSIAN FEDERATION
See Europe

TAJIKISTAN
Capital: Dushanbe
Population: 5,700,000
Area: 55,250 sq mi

TURKMENISTAN
Capital: Ashkhabad
Population: 4,000,000
Area: 188,500 sq mi

UZBEKISTAN
Capital: Tashkent
Population: 21,700,000
Area: 172,700 sq mi

THE FAR EAST

CHINA
[including Hong Kong]
Capital: Beijing
Population: 1,207,406,000
Area: 3,695,500 sq mi

JAPAN
Capital: Tokyo
Population: 124,959,000
Area: 145,884 sq mi

MACAO
[Portugal, reverts to Chinese rule in 1999]
Capital: Macao
Population: 374,000
Area: 7 sq mi

MONGOLIA
Capital: Ulan Bator
Population: 2,371,000
Area: 604,830 sq mi

NORTH KOREA
Capital: Pyongyang
Population: 23,054,000
Area: 46,540 sq mi

SOUTH KOREA
Capital: Seoul
Population: 44,200,000
Area: 38,328 sq mi

TAIWAN
Capital: Taipei
Population: 21,000,000
Area: 13,900 sq mi

SOUTHERN ASIA

BANGLADESH
Capital: Dhaka
Population: 122,210,000
Area: 56,977 sq mi

BHUTAN
Capital: Thimphu
Population: 1,700,000
Area: 18,000 sq mi

INDIA
Capital: New Delhi
Population: 903,000,000
Area: 1,222,243 sq mi

NEPAL
Capital: Kathmandu
Population: 21,086,000
Area: 56,827 sq mi

MALDIVES
Capital: Malé
Population: 239,000
Area: 115 sq mi

MYANMAR (BURMA)
Capital: Yangon (Rangoon)
Population: 44,613,000
Area: 261,218 sq mi

PAKISTAN
Capital: Islamabad
Population: 122,802,000
Area: 307,374 sq mi

SRI LANKA
Capital: Colombo
Population: 17,800,000
Area: 25,332 sq mi

SOUTH EAST ASIA

BRUNEI
Capital: Bandar Seri Begawan
Population: 280,000
Area: 2,226 sq mi

CAMBODIA
Capital: Phnomh Penh
Population: 12,000,000
Area: 69,898 sq mi

CHRISTMAS ISLAND
[Australia]
Capital: Flying Fish Cove
Population: 1,275
Area: 52 sq mi

COCOS (KEELING) ISLANDS
[Australia]
Capital: West Island
Population: 650
Area: 6 sq mi

INDONESIA
Capital: Jakarta
Population: 191,170,000
Area: 735,310 sq mi

LAOS
Capital: Vientiane
Population: 4,605,000
Area: 91,400 sq mi

MALAYSIA
Capital: Kuala Lumpur
Population: 19,239,000
Area: 127,320 sq mi

PHILIPPINES
Capital: Manila
Population: 65,650,000
Area: 120,000 sq mi

SINGAPORE
Capital: Singapore City
Population: 2,874,000
Area: 250 sq mi

THAILAND
Capital: Bangkok
Population: 58,584,000
Area: 198,115 sq mi

VIETNAM
Capital: Hanoi
Population: 70,902,000
Area: 128,066 sq mi

Armenia

Azerbaijan

Turkmenistan

Uzbekistan

Afghanistan

Tajikistan

Kazakstan

Kyrgyzstan

Pakistan

 China   **Myanmar (Burma)**  **Bhutan**   **Bangladesh**   **Nepal**   **Maldives**   **Sri Lanka**   **India**

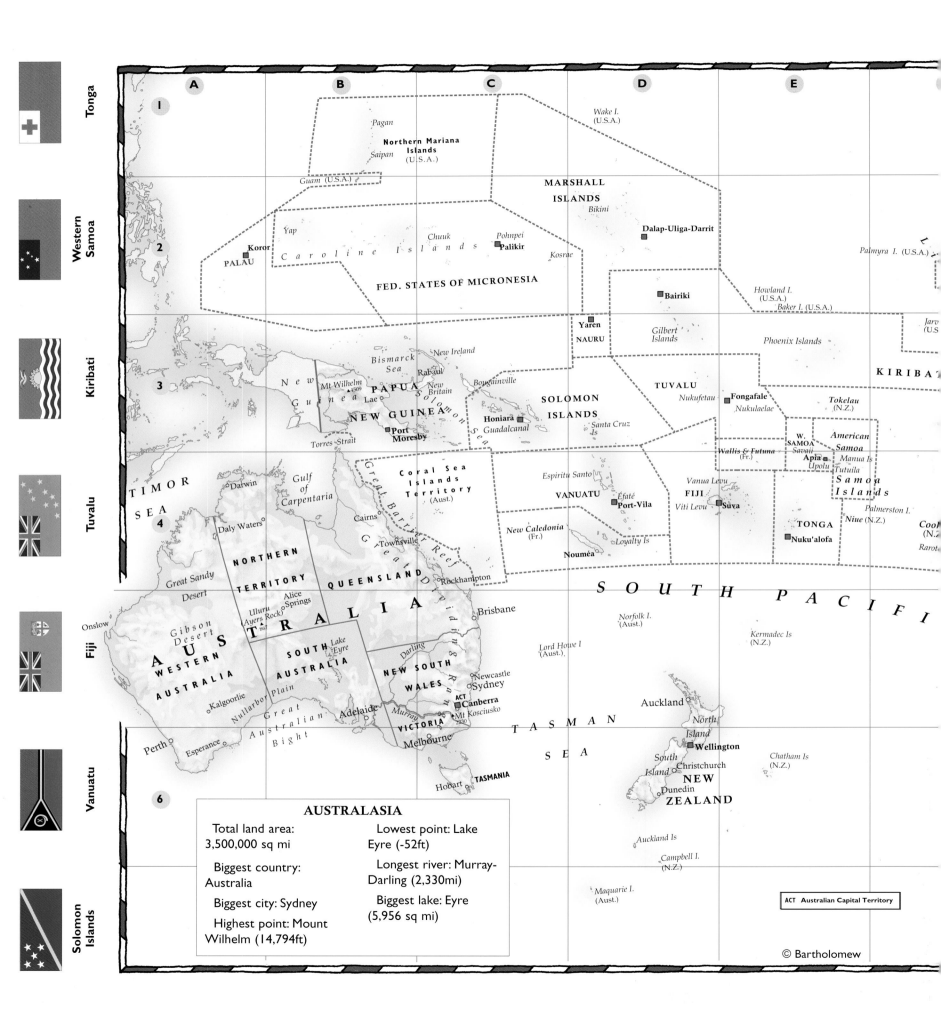

Tonga

Western Samoa

Kiribati

Tuvalu

Fiji

Vanuatu

Solomon Islands

A   B   C   D   E

1

Wake I.
(U.S.A.)

Pagan

Northern Mariana Islands
(U.S.A.)

Saipan

Guam (U.S.A.)

2

Yap

Koror
PALAU

Caroline Islands

Chuuk

Pohnpei
Palikir

Kosrae

MARSHALL ISLANDS

Bikini

Dalap-Uliga-Darrit

Palmyra I. (U.S.A.)

FED. STATES OF MICRONESIA

Bairiki

Howland I.
(U.S.A.)
Baker I. (U.S.A.)

Jarv
(U.S

3

Bismarck Sea

New Ireland

Rabaul

New
Guinea

Mt Wilhelm
4509

PAPUA

Lae

New
Britain

Bougainville

Solomon

NEW GUINEA

Port Moresby

Torres Strait

Honiara
Guadalcanal

SOLOMON ISLANDS

Santa Cruz
Is

Yaren
NAURU

Gilbert
Islands

Phoenix Islands

TUVALU

Nukufetau

Fongafale
Nukulaelae

Tokelau
(N.Z.)

K I R I B A T

**W.
SAMOA**
Savaii

**American
Samoa**

4

TIMOR

Darwin

Gulf
of
Carpentaria

SEA

Daly Waters

Coral Sea
Islands
Territory
(Aust.)

Espiritu Santo

VANUATU

Éfaté
Port-Vila

New Caledonia
(Fr.)

Nouméa

Loyalty Is

Vanua Levu

FIJI

Viti Levu

Suva

Apia
Upolu

Tutuila
Manua Is

**Samoa
Islands**

Palmerston I.

TONGA

Niue (N.Z.)

Nuku'alofa

Cairns

Great Barrier Reef

Townsville

Rockhampton

S O U T H   **P A C I F I**

Cool
(N.Z

Raro

5

Onslow

Great Sandy
Desert

Gibson
Desert

**NORTHERN
TERRITORY**

Alice
Springs

Uluru
(Ayers Rock)
867

QUEENSLAND

Great
Dividing
Range

Brisbane

Norfolk I.
(Aust.)

Kermadec Is
(N.Z.)

**WESTERN
AUSTRALIA**

A U S T R A L I A

Kalgoorlie

Lake
Eyre

**SOUTH
AUSTRALIA**

Darling

**NEW SOUTH
WALES**

Newcastle
Sydney

Lord Howe I
(Aust.)

Auckland

North
Island

Nullarbor Plain

Great

Australian

Bight

Adelaide

Murray

ACT Canberra
Mt Kosciusko
2230

VICTORIA

T A S M A N

S E A

Christchurch

South
Island

Wellington

Chatham Is
(N.Z.)

6

Perth

Esperance

Melbourne

Hobart **TASMANIA**

Dunedin

**NEW
ZEALAND**

Auckland Is

Campbell I.
(N.Z.)

Maquarie I.
(Aust.)

AUSTRALASIA

Total land area:
3,500,000 sq mi

Biggest country:
Australia

Biggest city: Sydney

Highest point: Mount
Wilhelm (14,794ft)

Lowest point: Lake
Eyre (-52ft)

Longest river: Murray-
Darling (2,330mi)

Biggest lake: Eyre
(5,956 sq mi)

ACT Australian Capital Territory

© Bartholomew

108

AUSTRALIA

Australia is an island so large that it is almost a continent. Most Australian cities are on the coast, while inland are vast deserts and empty bush country. Tropical Papua New Guinea lies to the the north, and temperate New Zealand to the east. Beyond lie the blue waters of the South Pacific, scattered with volcanic and coral islands. All these islands lie within the continent known as Australasia or Oceania.

AMERICAN SAMOA
[United States]
Capital: PagoPago
Population: 47,000
Area: 77 sq mi

AUSTRALIA
Capital: Canberra
Population: 17,800,000
Area: 2,966,200 sq mi

COOK ISLANDS
[New Zealand]
Capital: Avarua
Population: 19,000
Area: 91 sq mi

FEDERATED STATES OF MICRONESIA
Capital: Dalikir
Population: 114,000
Area: 271 sq mi

FIJI
Capital: Suva
Population: 758,000
Area: 7,095 sq mi

FRENCH POLYNESIA
[France]
Capital: Papeete
Population: 212,000
Area: 1,359 sq mi

GUAM
[United States]
Capital: Agaña
Population: 139,000
Area: 209 sq mi

KIRIBATI
Capital: Bairiki
Population: 77,000
Area: 313 sq mi

MARSHALL ISLANDS
Capital: Dalap-Uliga-Darrit
Population: 52,000
Area: 70 sq mi

NAURU
Main town: Yaren
Population: 10,000
Area: 8 sq mi

NEW CALEDONIA
[France]
Capital: Nouméa
Population: 179,000
Area: 7,358 sq mi

NEW ZEALAND
Capital: Wellington
Population: 3,490,000
Area: 104,454 sq mi

NIUE
[New Zealand]
Capital: Alofi
Population: 2,270
Area: 100 sq mi

NORFOLK ISLAND
[Australia]
Capital: Kingston
Population: 2,000
Area: 13 sq mi

NORTHERN MARIANA ISLANDS
[United States]
Capital: Saipan
Population: 43,500
Area: 184 sq mi

PALAU
Capital: Koror
Population: 16,000
Area: 188 sq mi

PAPUA NEW GUINEA
Capital: Port Moresby
Population: 4,056,000
Area: 178,704 sq mi

PITCAIRN ISLANDS
[United Kingdom]
Capital: Adamstown
Population: 71
Area: 16 sq mi

SOLOMON ISLANDS
Capital: Honiara
Population: 354,000
Area: 10,639 sq mi

TOKELAU
[New Zealand]
Population: 1,760
Area: 4 sq mi

TONGA
Capital: Nukualofa
Population: 105,000
Area: 290 sq mi

TUVALU
Capital: Fongafala
Population: 13,000
Area: 10 sq mi

VANUATU
Capital: Port-Vila
Population: 20,000
Area: 4,707 sq mi

WALLIS AND FUTUNA
[France]
Capital: Mata Uta
Population: 14,100
Area: 77 sq mi

WESTERN SAMOA
Capital: Apia
Population: 164,000
Area: 1,093 sq mi

LEFT: This small coral platform – covered in lush vegetation – is in the Vava'u group of islands which is part of the kingdom Tonga in the Pacific Ocean.

 Australia
 New Zealand
 Papua New Guinea
 Palau
 Fed States of Micronesia
 Marshall Islands
 Nauru

Marquesas Islands

Rangiroa *Tuamotu Archipelago*
Tahiti *French*
Society Islands *Hao*
Polynesia
Mururoa
Tubuai Islands *Îles Gambier*

Pitcairn I. (U.K.)

OCEAN

Malden I.
Starbuck I.
Kiritimati

109

THE POLES

The Poles are the coldest places on earth. The ocean around the North Pole is covered by thick ice. In the brief Arctic summer its fringes break up into great icebergs. The Antarctic Circle occupies the southernmost part of the globe. It too is permanently frozen with an ice cap that is nearly five kilometres thick in places. But, unlike the North Pole, the South Pole lies over land. Some indigenous peoples have made their home in the Arctic, whereas the Antarctic is populated only by visiting scientists.

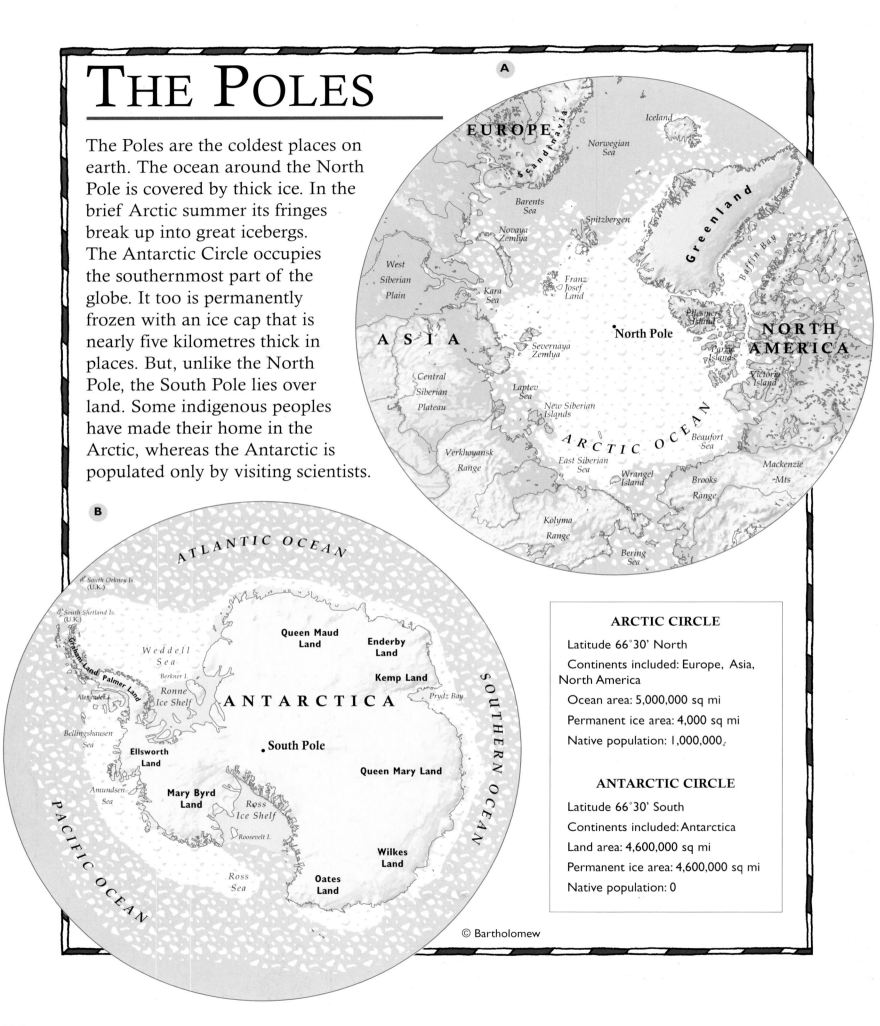

A

EUROPE
Scandinavia
Iceland
Norwegian Sea
Barents Sea
Spitzbergen
Novaya Zemlya
West Siberian Plain
Kara Sea
Franz Josef Land
Greenland
Baffin Bay
Ellesmere Island
ASIA
Severnaya Zemlya
North Pole
Parry Islands
NORTH AMERICA
Central Siberian Plateau
Laptev Sea
New Siberian Islands
Victoria Island
Verkhoyansk Range
East Siberian Sea
Wrangel Island
ARCTIC OCEAN
Beaufort Sea
Brooks Range
Mackenzie Mts
Kolyma Range
Bering Sea

B

ATLANTIC OCEAN
South Orkney Is. (U.K.)
South Shetland Is. (U.K.)
Weddell Sea
Queen Maud Land
Enderby Land
Graham Land
Palmer Land
Berkner I.
Ronne Ice Shelf
Kemp Land
Alexander I.
ANTARCTICA
Prydz Bay
Bellingshausen Sea
Ellsworth Land
South Pole
SOUTHERN OCEAN
Queen Mary Land
Amundsen Sea
Mary Byrd Land
Ross Ice Shelf
Roosevelt I.
Wilkes Land
Ross Sea
Oates Land
PACIFIC OCEAN

© Bartholomew

ARCTIC CIRCLE

Latitude 66°30' North

Continents included: Europe, Asia, North America

Ocean area: 5,000,000 sq mi

Permanent ice area: 4,000 sq mi

Native population: 1,000,000

ANTARCTIC CIRCLE

Latitude 66°30' South

Continents included: Antarctica

Land area: 4,600,000 sq mi

Permanent ice area: 4,600,000 sq mi

Native population: 0

SUBJECT INDEX

The publishers would like to thank the following artists for contributing to the book:

Cy Baker (Wildlife Art Agency), Simone Boni (Virgil Pomfret Agency), Joanne Cowne, Luigi Crittone (Virgil Pomfret Agency), William Donohoe, Richard Draper, Luigi Gallante (Virgil Pomfret Agency), Nick Harris (Virgil Pomfret Agency), Christian Hook, Hans Jenssen (Virgil Pomfret Agency), Sharon MacCausland, John Mack, Kevin Maddison, Chris Orr Associates, Malcolm Porter, Steve Roberts (Wildlife Art Agency), Mike Saunders, Peter Scott (Wildlife Art Agency), Hayley Simmons, Gill Thomblin, Phil Weare (Linden Artists), Ann Winterbotham.

The publishers would like to thank the following for providing photographs, and for granting permission to reproduce copyright material:

AKG London
69t, 74b, Erich Lessing 86t, 86bl
Bruce Coleman Ltd
Christer Frederiksson 12t, Hans-Peter Merten 18, Jules Cowan 8-9, 21 & 28t, Jens Rydell 23t, Erwin & Peggy Bauer 30t & 43, John Shaw 30m & 41, Konrad Wothe 31b, Fred Bruemmer 38t, Eckart Pott 38b & 56t, Gunter Ziesler 48t & 58t, Staffan Widstrand 49, Charles & Sandra Hood 55, George McCarthy 57, Peter Davey 62b, 79bl, Clive Hicks 69b, Staffan Widstrand 71t, Luiz Claudio Marigo 100b
James Davis Travel Photography
71b, 88, 89l, 100t
Ecoscene
42t, Sally Morgan 58b, Rik Schaffer 62m
ET Archive
72, 73t, 74t, 75b, 87tl, 91b
Eye Ubiquitous
89r
Freytag-Berndt & Artaria
94t
Geoscience Features Picture Library
Dr B Booth 12t, 13, JD Griggs 15t, 16t, 25t, W Hughes 27t, 31t
Hulton Getty
66t, 76, 77, 90m
Hutchison Library
T Page 17, Patricio Goycoolea 20t, Edward Parker 22, Vanessa S Boeye 46, Pern 81ml, 85b
The Mansell Collection
52t

Mary Evans Picture Library
33b, 60, 68, 73b, 74m, 75tl, 75tr, 84t
Henry Moore Foundation
Photo Michel Muller (reproduced by permission) 86br
Don Morley
50
NHPA
Julie Meech 15b, Haroldo Palo 18-19, Rich Kirchner 19t, Karl Switak 26t, Anthony Bannister 27b & 51, Kevin Schafer 36-37, 28b & 44, Ralph & Daphne Keller 29m, David Woodfall 35 & 62t, Stephen Dalton 41t, Jany Sauvanet 42b, Laurie Campbell 45, A N T 47, R Sovensen & J Olsen 53t, Peter Parks 53b, B Jones & M Shimlock 54, B & C Alexander 56b, Norbert Wu 59, Daniel Heuclin 61, Steve Robinson 66
Oxford Scientific Films
Stan Osolinski 30b, Fred Bavendam 52b, Belinda Wright 63
Popperfoto
26b, AFP 90b, Reuter 91m
Rex Features/SIPA Press
91t
Science Photo Library
NASA 10, Julian Baum 11, David Parker 12b, Joyce Photographics 19m, Ron Church 24, J G Golden 25m, Jack Finch 29t, NASA 31m, Richard Folwell 32, Russell D Curtis 33t, Jim Amos 61b, John Reader 66b, Sinclair Stammers 67, Earth Satellite Corporation 95
Still Pictures
Carlos Guarita 20b, Edward Parker 25b, Hartmut Schwarzbach 34, Mark Edwards 40, B & C Alexander 78t, Mark Edwards 78b, Jorgen Schytte 81b
Tony Stone Images
Andrew Errington 16b, John and Eliza Forder 23b, Tony Craddock 28b-29, Greg Pobst 39, Randy Wells 48m, Dennis Waugh 64-65, Andy Chadwick 70t, Ed Simpson 70b, Penny Tweedie 79t, David Hiser 79br, Ian Shaw 80, Jamey Stillings 81t, David Woodfall 81mr, David Sutherland 82, Bushnell/Soifer 83t, Sarah Stone 83b, Chris Speedie 84b, Trevor Wood 85t, Martin Rogers 90t, Jon Bradley 92-93, Kim Westerskov 109
The Tate Gallery, London
© Roy Lichtenstein/DACS 1997 87tr
TRIP
J Wakelin 29b, Eric Smith 79m, J Arnold 82b, 83ml, D Brooker 94b
ZEFA

48b, 83mr

While every effort has been made to trace and acknowledge all copyright holders, we would like to apologise should any omissions have been made.

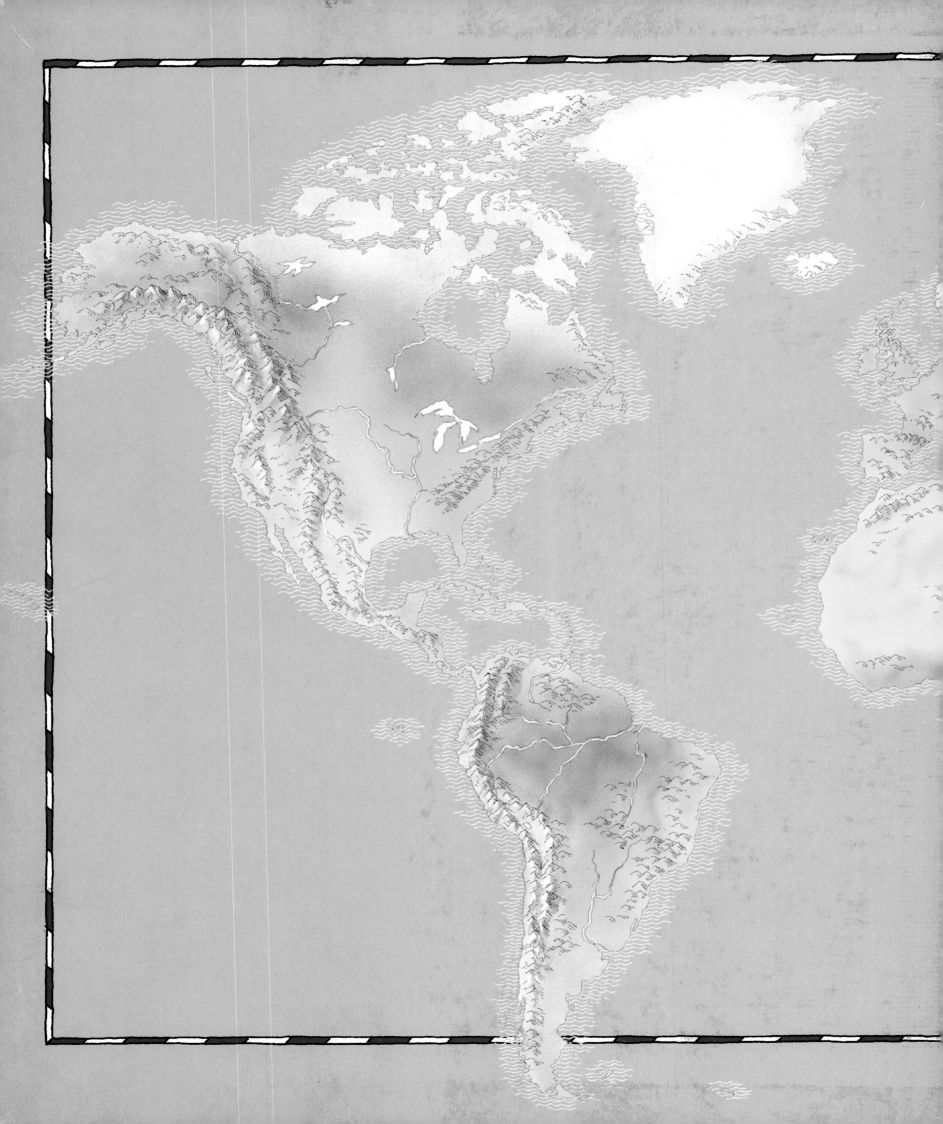